KOSOVO

INTERNATIONAL PEACE ACADEMY
OCCASIONAL PAPER SERIES

KOSOVO

An Unfinished Peace

William G. O'Neill

LYNNE
RIENNER
PUBLISHERS

BOULDER
LONDON

Published in the United States of America in 2002 by
Lynne Rienner Publishers, Inc.
1800 30th Street, Boulder, Colorado 80301
www.rienner.com

and in the United Kingdom by
Lynne Rienner Publishers, Inc.
3 Henrietta Street, Covent Garden, London WC2E 8LU

Library of Congress Cataloging-in-Publication Data
O'Neill, William G.
    Kosovo : an unfinished peace / William G. O'Neill.
        p. cm.—(International Peace Academy occasional paper series)
    Includes bibliographical references and index.
    ISBN 1-58826-021-6 (pbk. : alk. paper)
    1. Kosovo (Serbia)—History—Civil War, 1998—Peace.   2. Human
rights—Yugoslavia—Kosovo (Serbia).   3. Criminal justice, Administration
of—Yugoslavia—Kosovo (Serbia).   I. Title.   II. Series.
DR2087.6.P43 O54   2001
949.7103—dc21

                                                                  2001048121

British Cataloguing in Publication Data
A Cataloguing in Publication record for this book
is available from the British Library.

Printed and bound in the United States of America

     The paper used in this publication meets the requirements
∞   of the American National Standard for Permanence of
     Paper for Printed Library Materials Z39.48-1984.

     5   4   3   2   1

Contents

Foreword

David M. Malone,
President, International Peace Academy

We publish with great pride, in the International Peace Academy Occasional Paper Series, William G. O'Neill's fascinating volume on human rights in Kosovo as seen through the prism of his experience with the UN mission there in 1999–2000. This text builds on the efforts of the International Peace Academy to bring serious research and policy-development writing to scholars and practitioners alike. Importantly for the UN and other international organizations, Bill O'Neill provides both useful conclusions at the end of his text and some specific recommendations for a variety of actors.

Bill is well known to and widely admired within not only UN circles, but also the broader human rights and international legal communities to which he belongs. He served with distinction in the joint UN-OAS Civilian Mission in Haiti during the years 1993–1995 and in the UN's Human Rights Mission in Rwanda in 1995–1997. His field experience thus extends as broadly as his commitment to the protection and promotion of international human rights standards runs deep.

It is our hope that the events documented here and the reflections of the author will inspire the UN, regional organizations, governments, and nongovernmental organizations to consider not only what we need to do better in future international deployments, but also what we do well and on what existing "good practices" we can build.

We are deeply grateful to Bill for the in-depth research he carried out in preparation for the writing of this fluent and illuminating text, and for preparing the draft under tight deadlines. The result, we believe, fully justifies the effort involved.

He and we are most grateful to the Ford Foundation for funding the research and publication of this volume that aims above all, as usual with International Peace Academy work, at being policy relevant.

Preface

Working in Kosovo is a challenging and humbling experience, and the issues are complex and overwhelming. The suffering of the people of Kosovo and their ability to get on with life after losing so much is truly inspiring. The desire to hold the guilty accountable is praiseworthy, less so the thirst for vengeance held by some Kosovo Albanians.

I worked in Kosovo from September 1999 to March 2000 as the senior adviser on human rights to the special representative of the Secretary-General. Since then, I have stayed in virtual daily contact with former colleagues in the UN mission and with several Kosovar friends. All interviews conducted for this study occurred during a research trip I made to Kosovo in September 2000 and in subsequent meetings in New York and elsewhere. Unfortunately, due to the ongoing danger and violence in Kosovo, everyone I interviewed there asked that their names not be used, and I have honored their requests. Likewise, most UN and OSCE officials requested anonymity.

Concerning place names, I have decided to use the Serbian versions because these are more familiar and I did not want to burden the reader with the tiresome practice of repeating two names for every place, thus adding to an already lengthy work. My decision has no political content or intent, and in a few places I use the Albanian version where that has become widely known.

Although I did not begin this study with moral questions in mind, it soon became clear that Kosovo presents a complex moral universe. I tried to identify the moral challenges throughout the text. But one demands attention at the outset: is it morally right or responsible to expect that Kosovo Albanians and Kosovo Serbs reach some accommodation after the horrors of the past twelve years? Is it "starry-eyed naïveté" or "Western human rights–style neocolonialism" to promote tolerance and respect for diversity? Perhaps. But if so, I think it is the lesser of two evils. It is a serious misreading of the Balkans to assume that its inhabitants are congenitally incapable of coexistence or that alleged immutable and ancient ethnic hatreds require partitioning of territories and people. Worse, I think it is patronizing to conclude that Kosovars cannot distinguish between who is guilty of a crime against humanity and who is an innocent neighbor, or that mutual respect and honoring cultural diversity are unattainable goals. While the guilty must be punished and the past never forgotten, it would be morally irresponsible to accept pat explanations and demand anything less than an all-out effort to reach these goals.

—*William G. O'Neill*

Acknowledgments

Many people helped make this book possible. First, I want to thank the many good and brave people of all ethnic backgrounds from Kosovo. Unfortunately, they must remain anonymous, but their insights, honesty, and generosity were invaluable.

UNMIK and KFOR colleagues, too numerous to mention here, provided an example and an inspiration for all involved in modern peacekeeping operations. Staff at the International Peace Academy in New York, especially David Malone and Karin Wermester, provided substantive advice and administrative support.

I would also like to thank Katherine E. Garrett, David Malone, Ian Martin, Sandra Mitchell, and Elio Tamburi for their extremely helpful comments on earlier drafts. All mistakes, of course, are my responsibility.

This project would not have been possible without the generous support of the Ford Foundation. And I would never even have gone to Kosovo without the encouragement and backing of my wife, Katherine E. Garrett.

—W. G. O'N.

KOSOVO REGION

Map No. 4069 UNITED NATIONS
October 1998

Department of Public Information
Cartographic Section

1

Introduction

Snow and ice covered the road from Pristina to Obilic. It was another gray and freezing day in Kosovo in January 2000. Obilic, which houses Kosovo's two power plants, is ugly on a beautiful, sunny spring day but looked especially so in the dead of winter.

I had been working in Kosovo for about four months and I wanted to know more about what had happened during the 1998–1999 war. While Kosovo had never been a model of ethnic harmony, people lived in close proximity and usually did not kill or terrorize each other. In many cases, people had friends from other ethnic groups, played football together, and drank coffee in each other's houses.[1] Albanians in western Kosovo had a tradition of guarding Serb Orthodox holy sites and cemeteries.[2]

My interpreter seemed typical of many young Albanians: well educated and extremely curious about the world outside. While we often discussed life in the United States, on this day I decided to ask her some questions about the conflict and what she had seen.

Before the NATO bombing campaign began, she told me, she worked in Pristina and lived at home with her parents. Most of her friends were Albanian, but she also had a few Serb friends. Relations with the latter became more complex once the NATO bombing started, but she stayed close to one Serb friend who even brought her family food and water and offered to try to take them to a safer place if they wanted. The interpreter, whom I will call Carol, said that her friend was risking his life in offering such help.[3]

One day the Serb police came to Carol's apartment and told her and her parents that they had to leave immediately. The Serb regime was trying to empty part of Pristina of its Albanian population.[4] At the Macedonian border, Carol and her family joined the refugees whose pictures were broadcast around the world. Eventually, the family found refuge with relatives in the Macedonian capital of Skopje. After seventy-eight days of bombing,

A bombed oil refinery outside Pristina.

Milosevic agreed to pull his troops out of Kosovo, and Carol, her parents, and hundreds of thousands of Kosovo Albanians went home. It was the largest and most rapid refugee return in modern history.

Back in her parents' apartment in Pristina, Carol found work with the United Nations Interim Administration Mission in Kosovo (UNMIK) and started to contact her friends. Most were fine, but with spirits shaken by the violence and the loss of friends and relatives, they now wanted only to live normal, European lives and leave behind forever the cramped thinking and medieval attitudes that dominated Kosovo under the Serb regime.

She found a different situation facing her loyal Serb friend. He could not leave his flat; he had already received threats that his time "was up" in Kosovo. He was defiant; he told Carol that he was not afraid, that he had done nothing wrong; on the contrary, he had opposed Milosevic and had supported democracy and human rights, especially equal rights for all ethnic groups in Kosovo. But still the pressures against him escalated, culminating in threats on his life. He was in prison in his Pristina apartment but had not been tried or convicted of any crime. One day he left for Belgrade.

As Carol described her Serb friend's flight from Kosovo and the growing climate of hate, she became angry and frustrated. "This is not the kind of Kosovo we fought for during those ten years of Serb regime repression. This is not what I wanted, replacing one kind of ethnic domination by another." I asked her what we could do to build the Kosovo that she and her friends had risked their lives and futures for. Her answer was both shocking and discouraging: "I'm moving to Canada, I have applied for a visa. I am getting out of this place. I've had enough. I have family there and that is where my future is."

Kosovo cannot afford to lose its Carols. The young, educated, and talented are precisely the people needed to build a modern economy, a democratic government, and a tolerant, rights-respecting culture to ensure that Kosovo's youth can escape the ethnic hate that has periodically poisoned relations between communities.

Yet Kosovo has never had a better chance of breaking the cycle of violence and revenge and building a better future. With the departure of Milovsevic's military, police, and paramilitary forces, the most powerful military alliance on earth assumed control and responsibility for security. Over 40,000 heavily armed and highly trained troops, known as the Kosovo Force (KFOR) and led by NATO, took control. The United Nations Security Council, in Resolution 1244, gave the UN the authority to govern Kosovo while continuing to recognize that the Federal Republic of Yugoslavia maintained sovereignty over the territory. UNMIK was born, and thousands of international civil servants started to pour into Kosovo. Hundreds of nongovernmental organizations (NGOs) began the work of feeding, housing, and caring for the thousands who had lost everything. Here, finally, were some international actors who had the "power to do some good" that the English writer Rebecca West lamented had never been present in the Balkans.[5]

There is no doubt that for most residents of Kosovo, life is better today than it was during 1989–1999 when Serbia ruled Kosovo directly after stripping away its autonomy. This is a significant achievement. Many people, most of all Kosovo Albanians, have worked hard in difficult circumstances to restart lives shattered by oppression, violence, and finally war. Providing shelter, food and livestock, tools, building materials, and seeds as 800,000 traumatized refugees and 600,000 internally displaced persons returned home as a bitter Balkan winter awaited, is something for all who participated to be proud of. UNMIK, KFOR, and myriad international governmental and nongovernmental organizations and agencies have worked long hours in one of the largest international emergencies in recent times. Several soldiers and civilians have already paid with their lives for their efforts.

But something was going wrong. Yes, it was wonderful that Milosevic had finally yielded and that the brutal security forces had left. And yes, it was heartwarming to see Albanians returning to their homes and beginning to piece together their lives. Rebuilding began immediately; the sounds of hammers, cement mixers, and small generators reverberated throughout Kosovo. Fields, cleared of landmines, saw plows and seeds again. But there was also heartbreak at the death and destruction. Equally searing was the fate of those missing and those held in detention in prisons in Serbia proper.

My UN and KFOR colleagues and I were prepared for some acts of revenge against those responsible for inflicting such violence and pain and on the symbols of their power: government buildings and Serbian cultural sites, such as churches and monasteries. I had worked in Rwanda, where understandable yet still deplorable revenge occurred following the slaughter of at least 800,000 people in ninety days. But many of us were not prepared for the violence directed against virtually any Serb, Roma, or other non-Albanian—young or old. This violence began as quickly as the rebuilding efforts, during the first days in mid-June 1999 following NATO's entry into Kosovo. Distinctions were not made between people who may have been culpable for terrible crimes and innocent people like Carol's Serb friend.[6]

Some, including Kosovo Albanians, deplored the violence. Moreover, as months went by, the attacks continued and minorities were not the sole targets. As writer and editor Veton Surroi predicted when he criticized attacks against minorities in August 1999, Kosovo Albanians increasingly were targeted.[7] Surroi feared a creeping fascism taking hold. Murder, arson, robbery, beatings, and threats were directed against Albanians. These attacks had nothing to do with the so-called ancient ethnic hatreds of the Balkans or indeed with the recent atrocities committed by the Milosevic regime. Halil Dreshaj, a leading member of the moderate Democratic League of Kosovo (LDK), was killed when two gunmen wearing Kosovo Liberation Army (UCK) uniforms burst into his house and shot him in front of his family in June 2000.[8] On September 9, Marjan Melanosi, a journalist for Radio Television Kosovo was abducted after leaving work. The next day another Kosovo Albanian journalist, Shefki Popova, was murdered in Vucitrn. On September 11, Rexhep Luci was shot and killed in Pristina. He was director of city planning and a highly regarded architect. He had recently issued several demolition orders on illegal construction, which has plagued Pristina, and these orders obviously had offended some powerful people. Shefet Popova, an independent and highly regarded Kosovo Albanian journalist, was also murdered in September.

More overtly political was the murder of the LDK leader Ibrahim Rugova's senior political adviser, Xhemajl Mustafa, on November 23, 2000, in an ambush in the entry to his apartment in downtown Pristina. A week later, another LDK member, Ejup Visoka, was shot and seriously wounded as he drove his car in Podujevo. On December 15, another senior adviser to Rugova, Fetah Rudi, was shot and gravely wounded in the central town of Malisevo, a stronghold of Rugova's political adversary Hasim

Thaci. Rugova's LDK had recently trounced Thaci's party, the Democratic Party of Kosovo (PDK), and former UCK commander Ramush Haradinaj's Kosovo Alliance for the Future (AAK) in the October 28, 2000, elections. Political violence continued in 2001. On April 24, Ismet Raci, the president of the Klina municipality and a senior LDK official, was murdered in his apartment building. Six days earlier, a car bomb had killed one Serb and wounded several others as they left a building in Pristina that housed several Serb organizations.

How could KFOR try to stop the violence? What could the military do to protect the now endangered minorities and Albanian moderates? What was the best way to deal with the UCK and its efforts to take power? Could the UCK be marginalized without generating a backlash that could threaten KFOR itself? How could UNMIK tackle ongoing and past human rights abuses? What was the best way to get the legal system working? What challenges did UNMIK face in establishing law and order? How could the UN's International Civilian Police (CIVPOL) work effectively in this volatile environment? What was the best way to create a new Kosovo police force? What about human rights education? How could children learn about their rights and the rights of others? Was it too early to talk about some type of reconciliation, and if yes, what could we do in the meantime to promote tolerance and respect for human rights? How could UNMIK and KFOR harness this rare chance to use the "power to do good" to benefit the greatest number of people in Kosovo whatever their ethnicity?

I try to answer these questions in this book. In doing so, I first examine how the evolution of the UCK and the nature of the conflict between it and the Serb forces in the late 1990s has had enduring negative consequences for building respect for human rights, tolerance, and the rule of law in Kosovo today.

Next, I analyze the place of the Kosovo conflict in the context of the UN Security Council's interests in 1998–1999, especially the United States' role and how Kosovo overshadowed other, arguably more deadly, conflicts. This leads to the conclusion that Kosovo was not purely a humanitarian intervention but that it engaged certain national interests of the major powers.

I then describe the structure and mandate of both UNMIK and KFOR, the two dominant institutions representing the Security Council's response to the Kosovo crisis. Next I analyze the human rights situation in Kosovo under UNMIK and KFOR's watch and examine the role and responsibility of the UCK for ongoing violence against minorities and moderate Albanians. I argue that this is a direct result of the UCK's behavior during the previous struggle with Serb forces. The evidence in this section demonstrates something long denied by many in UNMIK and KFOR: the systematic and organized nature of the current violence against minorities and moderates.

This flawed analysis stemmed from UNMIK's and KFOR's failure to craft a forceful policy based on a nuanced analysis of the violence in Kosovo. Unfortunately, UNMIK and KFOR formulated a weak policy based on a simplistic analysis, refusing to discern between those working for stability versus those promoting violence. UNMIK and KFOR lacked the political will to control Albanian and Serbian extremists, caving in to their demands and allowing them to shape and control the agenda. I show how this soft approach has created serious obstacles to law and order, allowed an unacceptable level of violence in Kosovo, and enabled two insurgencies on its borders with Serbia proper and Macedonia to flourish. I also highlight several successful UNMIK and KFOR initiatives to protect human rights and physical security.

The following chapters take an in-depth look at three key areas: judicial reform, police work, and penal administration. I argue that for UNMIK and KFOR to accomplish their missions, getting a free and independent judiciary up and running and creating a multiethnic, rights-respecting police force are absolutely essential. UNMIK leadership valued political correctness, refusing to recognize the need for international jurists to counter blatant ethnic bias in the judiciary that jeopardized the success of legal reform. This reinforces Chilean human rights expert José Zalaquette's insight that "however much a decisive defeat of the perpetrators of grave crimes is to be desired, a victor's unfettered power creates, as history shows, a situation that is in itself a danger against justice."[9] I then analyze how the successor force to the UCK, the Kosovo Protection Corps (TMK), threatens stability.

In treating the crucial but often overlooked area of human rights education and promotion, I argue that human rights promotion is one of the strongest tools to prevent future human rights violations but that this is a long-term project and locals must take the lead in defining and designing this work.

I do not analyze in depth the ten years of Serb rule in Kosovo, nor do I examine even earlier periods of conflict over who should "rule" Kosovo.[10] I do not cover the debate over the legality of the NATO bombing campaign; much has been written about this topic. The legal issues are complex, but I find the moral complexities of postwar Kosovo more compelling.

Adam Roberts, professor of international relations at Oxford University, captures the moral dilemma of Kosovo succinctly:

> The fact that the campaign failed in the intended manner to avert a humanitarian disaster in the short term, even though it did eventually stop

it, makes it a questionable model of humanitarian intervention. The uncomfortable paradox involved—that a military campaign against ethnic cleansing culminated in a settlement in which the majority of Serbs resident in Kosovo departed—must reinforce the sense that humanitarian operations cannot suddenly transform a political landscape full of moral complexity.[11]

It is this moral complexity that bedevils UNMIK and KFOR efforts to stem violence and craft strategies to protect human rights. Failure means that people like Carol, her Serbian friend, and moderates of every ethnicity will flee, leaving behind an intolerant and violent Kosovo.

NOTES

1. For a fascinating look at life in Kosovo in the 1960s and 1970s, see Mary Motes, *Kosova/Kosovo: Prelude to War, 1966–1999* (Homestead, Fla.: Redland Press, 1999). Motes lived and taught in Kosovo for long stretches in this period, one of the rare Westerners to do so. She ends her book in June 1999 with one of her Kosovo Albanian friends in Pristina saying, "I told my Serbian neighbors you must not go . . . Our neighbors were wonderful . . . They are marvelous, marvelous people . . . and I don't want them to go" (p. 308).

2. Miranda Vickers, *Between Serb and Albanian: A History of Kosovo* (New York: Columbia University Press, 1998, pp. xii, 27.

3. There are similar stories: "Our Serbian neighbors saved us. They are wonderful people. You know the old professor of psychology? He saved everyone on his floor. He said 'I am Serb and a writer. And if you touch anyone of these people I will write it all down.'" Motes, *Kosova/Kosovo*, p. 307.

4. Tim Judah, *Kosovo: War and Revenge* (New Haven: Yale University Press, 2000). Judah describes the Serb regime's strategy of ethnic cleansing, the so-called Operation Horseshoe (pp. 241–254). He also describes instances where Serbs acted much less heroically towards their Albanian friends and neighbors. "Those Serbs were our neighbors. We never had any problems with them, played with them, and ate with them. But, when the Serbian police came and burned our houses they turned their backs and said, 'Fuck you'" (p. ix). Others state that sometimes their former Serbian neighbors participated in ethnic cleansing. See Human Rights Watch, *Abuses Against Serbs and Roma in the New Kosovo* (New York: Human Rights Watch, August 1999), p. 5.

5. Rebecca West, *Black Lamb and Grey Falcon* (New York: Penguin, 1994), p. 913. West, notoriously pro-Serb, visited the region in the 1930s and despaired of any end to violence in the Balkans.

6. Some argue that the divide between Serbs and Albanians is too deep and that even minimal coexistence is unlikely. See David Rohde, "Kosovo Seething," *Foreign Affairs* 79, no. 3 (May/June 2000): 65–79. I disagree. Albanians I have spoken to want those Serbs responsible for crimes punished; but most oppose violence and said they could live again with those who did not participate in the ethnic cleansing. Likewise, many Serbs want to return to Kosovo and live with their Albanian neighbors. See UNMIK Press Briefings, February 19, 2001. Available at www.un.org/peace/kosovo/briefing/pressbriefing19Feb01.

7. Surroi's condemnation of the violence against minorities was published in

Koha Ditore, an Albanian language daily that Surroi publishes. His criticism was immediately answered by the Kosova Press Agency, which accused Surroi and his editor, Baton Haxhiu, of being "spies for Serbs" and for engaging in "pro-Serbian vampirism" and questioned whether they were "of Albanian blood." The Kosova Press Agency, a mouthpiece of the UCK, then said, "They may get killed and it will be understandable." See Anna Husarska, "Kosovo's New Witch Hunt," *Washington Post,* October 25, 1999, p. A29.

8. "Gunmen Kill Albanian Politician," Associated Press, June 16, 2000.

9. José Zalaquette, "Moral Reconstruction in the Wake of War Crimes," in Jonathan Moore, ed., *Hard Choices: Moral Dilemmas in Humanitarian Intervention* (Lanham Md.: Rowman and Littlefield Publishers, 1998), p. 214.

10. These periods are important for understanding what is happening now and are covered in several excellent works. Two of the best are Noel Malcolm's *A Short History of Kosovo* (New York: New York University Press, 1999), and Tim Judah's *The Serbs* (New Haven: Yale University Press, 1997).

11. Adam Roberts, "NATO's 'Humanitarian War' over Kosovo," *Survival: The IISS Quarterly* 41, no. 3 (autumn 1999): 102, 120.

2

Violence Gradually Prevails: The Prewar Period, 1989–1999

LOST AUTONOMY AND PASSIVE RESISTANCE, 1989–1995

After Slobodan Milosevic stripped Kosovo of its status as an autonomous region of Serbia in 1989, Kosovo Albanians reacted by beginning a program of passive resistance.[1] The Serb government forced many Kosovo Albanians from their jobs, completely altered the system of education by imposing the Serbian curriculum on everyone, and enacted many discriminatory laws. One of the most egregious was a law forbidding the transfer of real property from a Serb to an Albanian. This was an early indication of Milosevic's plan to alter the ethnic balance of Kosovo, which was overwhelmingly Albanian. Milosevic and other Serb extremists even talked of "demographic genocide" to describe the relatively high Albanian birthrate in Kosovo and the ever increasing Albanian share of Kosovo's population, coupled with Serb emigration.

Ibrahim Rugova, usually described as a mild-mannered professor wearing a silk scarf, emerged as the leader of Kosovo Albanians. Rugova, one of the founders of the LDK in 1989, preached passive resistance as the best way to achieve independence, the goal of the overwhelming majority of Albanians. Kosovo Albanians asked if 600,000 Montenegrins could have their own republic, why couldn't 2 million Kosovo Albanians?[2]

Money poured in from the large Kosovo Albanian diaspora in Western Europe and North America. The LDK party also imposed a 3 percent tax on all Albanians to help pay for the burgeoning services. This tax, while nominally voluntary, did have an element of coercion. The Kosovo Albanians set up their own schools and medical clinics. The pre-1989 school curriculum was used, and tens of thousands of children attended classes in houses and makeshift rooms. Doctors examined patients in basement clinics. A parallel society developed and Kosovo Albanians had limited contact with official state organs.[3] The police and court systems were almost entirely Serbian, which would have a major impact on postconflict Kosovo. But in general, Rugova's passive resistance strategy predominated with little violence or militancy in Kosovo from 1989 to 1995.

The strategy changed dramatically after the Dayton Peace Accords were signed in 1995, which ended the war in Bosnia. Milosevic attended the meetings in Dayton, Ohio, and signed the agreement on behalf of the Bosnian Serbs. Kosovo Albanians expected the conference to address their demands also. These expectations were unrealistic; Richard Holbrooke, who led the U.S. delegation and who was the prime mover in the talks, insists that the only issue on the agenda was a peaceful resolution to the war in Bosnia. Kosovo would have to wait.[4]

The complete avoidance of the Kosovo issue during the Dayton talks devastated the Albanians. Six years of passive resistance had nothing to show; some started to criticize Rugova's strategy for the first time in public. Kosovo Albanians could not help but notice that Bosnian Serbs received a form of territorial recognition in the Dayton Peace Accords with the creation of the Republika Srpska along with the Bosnian Muslim–Croatian Federation (which includes the Muslim and Croatian areas) within the Bosnian state. Some Albanians concluded that maybe violence did pay, while nonviolent resistance got you nowhere.

Shadowy groups of Kosovo Albanian exiles had operated in Western Europe for years. Some were disciples of Enver Hoxha, the long-term dictator in Albania. And it was events in Albania shortly after the disappointment of Dayton that changed the way Kosovo Albanians would fight for their independence; and those events would have a huge impact on the "moral complexity" of Kosovo following the NATO air campaign.

In the spring of 1997, a classic Ponzi pyramid financial scandal rocked Albania. Thousands of people, bilked of their meager life savings, poured into the streets and demanded government compensation. Desperate people, angry and frustrated with the lack of government action, started to raid army and police weapons depots all over the country. Soon, tens of thousands of Kalishnikovs and other automatic weapons, along with hundreds of thousands of rounds of ammunition, circulated throughout the country. This was a godsend to the nascent constellation of small Kosovo Albanian armed groups, who, unhappy with Rugova's policy of passive resistance, had recently launched violent attacks against selected Serb targets. What they most lacked was money and weaponry, and now thanks to the chaos in Albania, they suddenly had virtually unlimited access to both.

THE UCK EMERGES, 1995–1998

The Kosovo Liberation Army was founded in 1993 and grew as small, often squabbling groups gradually coalesced.[5] From 1993 to 1997, some

UCK members had gone to secret camps in Albania to receive military training; several raids into Kosovo occurred in this period, especially targeting isolated Serb police posts. The first UCK fighter to die in uniform is believed to have been Adrian Krasniqi, who was killed attacking a police station in western Kosovo in October 1997.[6] But with the disappointment of Dayton and the sudden availability of weapons from Albania at the beginning of 1998, the character and intensity of the armed resistance in Kosovo changed.

The Drenica Valley in central Kosovo had always strongly resisted Serb rule. Legendary nineteenth-century Kosovo Albanian guerrillas had come from this area. Among their modern descendants were the Jashari family of the village of Donji Prekaz. Adem Jashari was one of the small number of fighters who had gone to Albania for military training in 1990. Serb police, aware of this, had tried to arrest him on his return from Albania, but after a long gun battle, the police retreated and did not return. The Jasharis had succeeded in creating a "no-go" area for Serb police, and neighbors regarded them as heroes.[7]

After several high-profile attacks on Serb police in the Drenica Valley, and a funeral attended by 20,000 for a slain teacher killed by a stray bullet during a UCK attack on a Serb police patrol, the Serb police tried once again to arrest Adem Jashari and his supporters in Donji Prekaz. In January 1998, the police came, but the Jasharis resisted with help from their neighbors. After a police ambush on the UCK on February 28, 1998, and an ensuing firefight left several UCK and Serb police dead, the Serb police attacked several nearby families and killed numerous civilians, including women and children. On March 5, they decided to attack the Jashari family compound again. This time they used artillery and other heavy weapons. According to Human Rights Watch, fifty-eight people died, including eighteen women and ten children.[8] The Serb police had finally killed Adem Jashari, but Ibrahim Rugova's strategy to gain Kosovo's independence by passive resistance had been overtaken by events. Now the men with the guns would decide Kosovo's future. The Milosevic regime had failed to solve the "classic conundrum of how to suppress the insurgents without acting as their recruiting sergeants."[9]

The UCK, while still a numerically small group, grew increasingly bold. Sporadic attacks became increasingly common and coordinated. The major Western powers now started to panic as the possibility of everyone's nightmare scenario—war in Kosovo—became a possibility. Not forgotten, least of all by Kosovo Albanians, was then president George Bush's warning in December 1992 that "in the event of a conflict caused by Serbian action, the United States will be prepared to employ military force against the Serbians in Kosovo and in Serbia proper." President Bill Clinton repeated this warning on taking office, as did his first secretary of state, Warren Christopher. Robert Gelbard, President Clinton's special envoy to the

Balkans, rushed to see Milosevic to reiterate this message. Gelbard had visited Pristina just the previous month, in February 1998, and had condemned the growing violence by the Serbian police. He also denounced the UCK, stating, "We condemn very strongly terrorist actions in Kosovo. The UCK is, without any questions, a terrorist group."[10] The State Department had also classified the UCK as a terrorist organization in 1998. In his meeting with Milosevic, Gelbard noted that by killing innocent civilians in Drenica, Milosevic had "done more than anyone to increase the membership of the UCK."[11] Yet some observers question whether Gelbard's condemnation of the UCK as terrorists was interpreted by Milosevic as a green light to unleash the Serbian police in the Drenica Valley barely ten days later, resulting in the killing of Adem Jashari and his family.

The UCK attacked police and occasionally Serb civilians throughout 1998, provoking swift, often disproportionate, Serb reprisals. Tensions increased, police roadblocks sprang up, and already fragile interethnic relations frayed further. During the summer of 1998, Serb forces launched a major offensive to crush the UCK and to recapture the Drenica Valley, causing the first large-scale exodus of Albanians from their villages to the hills. Western efforts to hold talks between the Albanians and Milosevic failed, primarily because the UCK rejected any negotiations with Belgrade.[12] Urgent action to head off a full-scale conflict was needed; winter was approaching and thousands of people would die if they had to remain without adequate food or shelter in the hills. Balkan troubleshooter Richard Holbrooke returned at President Clinton's request to find a solution to the Kosovo crisis.

NATO threatened Milosevic with air strikes if he did not halt his attacks on civilians. With this threat as his main bargaining chip, Holbrooke secured Milosevic's agreement in October 1998 to withdraw most of his forces and, most important, to allow the deployment of 2,000 unarmed international inspectors to verify compliance with the agreement as a "confidence-building measure" for the civilian population. This mission was called the Kosovo Verification Mission, or KVM.

THE KOSOVO VERIFICATION MISSION, OCTOBER 1998–JUNE 1999

The KVM was established on October 16, 1998. Composed primarily of former or active-duty military officers serving in a civilian capacity, they came from the member states of the Organization for Security and Cooperation in Europe (OSCE). The KVM never reached its mandated number of 2,000; the maximum deployed before its evacuation in March 1999 was about 1,200. The KVM's mission was to monitor compliance with UN Security Council Resolution 1199, which called for an immediate cease-fire, and "the withdrawal of security units used for civilian repression."

KVM monitors deployed gradually all over Kosovo. A Human Rights Division was established to "monitor, investigate, document and report on allegations of human rights abuses by all parties to the conflict in Kosovo."[13] These were primarily civilians with expertise in human rights and the laws of armed conflict. KVM human rights officers compiled daily and weekly reports while they were in Kosovo and conducted extensive interviews with thousands of refugees after the KVM was evacuated in March, days before the NATO air campaign began. A review of their reports shows a clear, organized, and brutal campaign by Serb forces to intimidate the Albanian population; KVM also believed that Milosevic was planning to expel this population based on Operation Horseshoe long before the NATO air campaign began on March 24, 1999.

The KVM's analysis of the conflict from the October 1998 agreement to the end of the bombing in June 1999 demonstrates why UNMIK and KFOR have such a difficult task protecting minorities and creating the rule of law in Kosovo now.

First, the violence perpetrated against Albanians was planned and organized at the highest levels of Serbian authority. The Serb army, police, and paramilitaries were not rogue actors, "out of control" and carrying out their own personal vendettas. There was no breakdown in command and control.

Second, the Serb army (VJ), police (MUP), and various paramilitary forces (most of whose members were recruited outside Kosovo with many coming from Bosnia) specifically targeted various segments of Kosovo Albanian society. Most at risk were young men of fighting age; all were deemed as actual or potential members of the UCK. Intellectuals, community and religious leaders, politicians, medical professionals, journalists, teachers and students, and human rights activists suffered serious human rights violations. The KVM documented numerous cases of summary executions, torture, arbitrary detention, and denial of access to basic public services.[14] After the KVM evacuated from Kosovo on March 20, 1999, some of its local Albanian staff were targeted by the Serb forces; several were killed, more were beaten or harassed, and some had their homes destroyed.

Third, sexual crimes against women and young girls were widespread. The KVM noted that the pattern of violence against Albanian women differed in important respects from the attacks against men.

> Much of the violence that women suffered seems to have been directed towards their gender in a way that appears also to have been intended to

humiliate the whole of Kosovo Albanian society. Instead of being arbitrar-
ily killed, as were many men, many women suffered rape and other forms
of sexual violence, since the perpetrators knew that this attached extreme
stigma in many women's eyes.[15]

This violence has had a lasting impact on Kosovo society. The number of
female-headed households is very high. Since men are the traditional
breadwinners in Kosovo Albanian society, many of these families are desti-
tute. Some raped women have been shunned or rejected by their husbands
and families and face no realistic hope of remarrying.[16] This humiliation
was precisely one of the goals of the Serb forces' violence. Finally, domestic violence is a serious problem in Kosovo today. This is common after
such systematic sexual violence.

Children were not spared either. Young girls were raped, according to
the KVM; some young boys were killed since they might grow up to be
guerrilla fighters. As we have seen, Serb forces' reprisal attacks on suspected UCK outposts were brutal and often did not discriminate between com-
batant and civilian. Children, even if not targeted, sometimes were killed in
the hail of bullets, grenades, and artillery. As NATO bombing intensified,
the blanket Serb military and police reprisals intensified. One example captures this terrible and deadly dynamic:

> Serb paramilitary forces who entered the village of Zulfaj [near Djakova]
> on 5 April 1999, irritated by the cries of terrified children as they searched
> the house before expelling inhabitants and torching the houses said, "You
> wanted NATO, now you got them! As long as they kill our children, we
> will kill yours."[17]

Children also witnessed scenes of unimaginable horror. Some saw their
parents killed before their eyes. Others saw relatives, friends, or neighbors
killed, beaten, or humiliated. The almost constant tension arising from military, police, and paramilitary patrols and roadblocks disrupted everyday life
and soon became "normal" for all children in Kosovo. The long-term effect
of these traumatic experiences on Kosovo's children, but particularly within the Albanian community—which suffered disproportionately—is only
now being realized. As we will see, children are committing ethnically
motivated crimes in Kosovo. The violence they witnessed and suffered has
complicated efforts to promote respect for diversity and tolerance.

AN OVERVIEW OF UCK CONDUCT DURING THE CONFLICT

The OSCE/KVM reports also include violations committed by the UCK
against Serbs and other minorities, and also against other Albanians whom

it suspected of "collaborating" with the Serb regime. I am not saying that there is some kind of "equivalence" in scale of violations, nor am I seeking to establish "balance" in assessing the violence. There is no equivalence and there is no balance; Albanians suffered enormously as a direct result of official Yugoslav/Serbian government policy. The Serb forces committed many more atrocities than did the UCK. It would be dishonest, however, to pretend that the UCK did not commit violations of human rights and humanitarian law; these violations complicate current efforts to enhance security and human rights in Kosovo.

Moreover, the UCK violence fed into a dynamic that ratcheted up the level of suffering for Kosovo Albanians. This raises complex moral issues: to what extent are the UCK partially responsible when they knew that by attacking Serbs the reprisals would be swift and disproportionate, directed against innocent members of the Albanian community?[18] The UCK counted on the Serbs to respond by attacking Albanian civilians, thereby triggering international outrage and an international military intervention to end Serb rule in the province.[19] Amazingly, this strategy ultimately worked, but not before several thousand people were killed and hundreds of thousands were displaced from their homes.[20]

And to what extent must the West answer because it never seriously tried to restrain the UCK from provoking the Serbs or identified ways to restrain the Serbs' violent response, thus helping ensure a NATO intervention to fight a war on behalf of the UCK that it could never have won alone? What is NATO's and the European Union's responsibility in failing to support more meaningful efforts to resolve the Kosovo crisis peacefully so that Kosovo Albanians would not have to conclude that the only way to self-governance flowed from the barrel of a gun?

The United States assisted the UCK in 1998 and 1999 and accepted them as the "ground troops" that the United States and NATO countries did not want to deploy themselves.[21] Supreme Allied Commander General Wesley Clark makes this point vividly clear in his memoirs when talking about the effort to support the UCK in holding the strategic heights of Mount Pastrik against a Serb counteroffensive. "That mountain is not going to be lost. We're not having Serbs on the top of that mountain. We'll have to pay for the top of that hill with American blood if we don't help the KLA hold it now."[22] After the bombing, the international community has had to work with the UCK and, since its formal dissolution in September 1999, with its former leaders and cadres, many of whom have "unclean hands." The current violence against the Serbs, Roma, Muslim Slavs, and Albanian moderates occurs while Kosovo is a ward of the UN and NATO. This violence has its roots in the 1998–1999 conflict and must be recognized if UNMIK, NATO, and, most important, the people of Kosovo are to craft solutions ending violence and preventing future abuses.

KVM mission reports throughout this period illustrate the pattern of violence. A report from early March 1999 notes that neither side shows it is interested in deescalating violence or adhering to the strictures of UN Security Council Resolution 1199. "Unprovoked KLA [UCK] attacks on police continue and their casualties have increased, while the number of VJ [Serbian police] deployed outside their barracks has increased."[23]

Another sinister development was the execution of Kosovo Albanians; in March 1999 alone, ten Albanian males were found shot dead with a single bullet to the head near Pec and Djakovica. They were suspected of being "loyal" to the Serb regime, and the conclusion is that the UCK police executed them.[24] The UCK formed a police force known as the PU, which arrested and detained people. It detained Albanians deemed too "friendly" with either the Serb regime or their Serb neighbors. The KVM monitors detected increased policing by the UCK and "liquidation" of alleged Albanian collaborators, with growing evidence that the UCK were responsible for these attacks.

The KVM also noted that in late 1998 the UCK was showing signs of increased organization and coherence. Battalions and brigades were assigned numbers instead of village designations. Evidence emerged that geographically dispersed forces were sharing information and using similar terminology.[25] This finding is important because the extent of the UCK's organization, command, and control has become a key question in the post-conflict phase. Apologists for the violence after NATO's entry said that it stemmed from "rogue" elements acting independently and over whom the UCK leadership had no control. The KVM rejected a similar finding in March 1999, noting that "we conclude that some punishment shootings are ordered at the highest level of KLA [UCK] command."[26]

In March 1999, as the negotiations for a political solution continued in Rambouillet, France, the violence intensified. The VJ arrested scores of Albanian men of fighting age, often severely beating them before their release; they also burned houses and forced Albanians from their homes. The UCK, meanwhile, initiated numerous attacks against the police, killing twelve and wounding thirty-five others. Eyewitnesses reported that a UCK unit abducted Albanians working with the Serb police.

This illustrates one of the most contentious issues then and now in Kosovo: the fate of missing persons. During the height of the conflict, an unknown number of people "disappeared." Most were Albanians, but Serbs and Roma also went missing. A KVM report, citing figures from the International Committee of the Red Cross (ICRC), states that 146 people were reportedly abducted by the UCK or went missing in areas under UCK control.[27] Some of these may have been Albanians suspected of collaborating. About forty-eight Serbs had disappeared from the Orahovac area during intense fighting in the summer of 1998 before the KVM deployment.

KVM established a Committee on the Missing to work on the question of missing persons and abductions from both sides in the Orahovac area. Members came from both the Serb and Albanian communities, and the committee obtained some information on Albanians killed during the July 1998 fighting.[28] It was a good but unusual example of interethnic cooperation during the conflict.

The UCK consistently denied holding anyone in detention, and it was extremely difficult to determine the number, location, or status of the missing. This meant that the abductions had a terrifying effect on the Serb community. The issue of the missing complicated the already difficult relationship between the KVM and the Serb community, as it would later for UNMIK and the Albanian community. "The issue of the missing persons is increasingly becoming a major focal point for the Human Rights Office," the KVM noted.[29] While devoting much attention to the problem, little progress occurred before the KVM's evacuation four days before the NATO bombing campaign started on March 24, 1999. In an earlier meeting with Adem Demaci, a leading figure in the Kosovo Albanian community and chief spokesperson for the UCK, Demaci stated that he doubted any abducted Serbs would still be alive.[30]

The international negotiators overlooked or underestimated the importance of this issue in the negotiations in Kumanovo, Macedonia, in June 1999, which ended the NATO campaign.[31] An earlier draft of the Military Technical Agreement had contained a provision requiring the Serbs to account for all missing Albanians and release those detained, but this was dropped before the final text was agreed.[32] This omission later undermined security in Kosovo; the fate of missing persons and detainees fueled street demonstrations, sit-ins, and attacks on minorities, thus complicating efforts to promote reconciliation and multi-ethnicity. Yet the KVM had signaled the importance of the missing persons issue to all sides back in February, noting that "a political settlement will have to deal with this issue . . . a robust mandate is needed to determine the fate of the missing."[33] The Rambouillet Agreement also called for the return of all abducted persons and those held without charge and stated that each side shall provide information on the missing. Unfortunately, Security Council Resolution 1244 also failed to address the problem.

REALPOLITIK'S REAL EFFECTS: SECURITY COUNCIL IN ACTION

Resolution 1244 became the governing charter of Kosovo on June 10, 1999; Serb military, police, and paramilitaries withdrew almost simultaneously and KFOR entered on June 12. The resolution reflects numerous compromises. At the heart of the compromises, or the "mother of all compromises," according to one UN official, is the clear-as-mud treatment of Kosovo's future political status.

The resolution reaffirms both the UN's commitment to the territorial integrity of the Federal Republic of Yugoslavia (FRY) and the call for substantial autonomy and meaningful self-administration for Kosovo.[34] No one knew what the terms "substantial autonomy" and "meaningful self-administration" really meant. What united all Kosovo Albanians, regardless of their political party loyalties, was full independence from Serbia and what was left of the FRY. They did not want to hear about autonomy, however defined. A change in regime in Belgrade was also not sufficient; some Albanians said that Mahatma Gandhi, if he were alive, could become the president of Yugoslavia and they would still want independence. This overwhelming sentiment was confirmed about sixteen months later when Vojislav Kostunica became president of Yugoslavia, ousting Milosevic. The Albanian leadership and press in Kosovo virtually ignored the momentous change in Belgrade in October 2000, maintaining that whatever happened in Serbia had no bearing at all in Kosovo.

Security Council Resolution 1244 could not mention independence for Kosovo because most members of the council opposed any change in borders resulting from armed conflict, or otherwise. They did not want Kosovo to become a precedent for those agitating for independence. Some European member states also feared outright independence for Kosovo, citing fears of regional instability that could affect the Balkans from Turkey to Greece.

Resolution 1244's ambiguity on Kosovo's future has complicated UNMIK's and NATO's work. It also reinforced extremist views in both Albanian and Serb camps, undermining security and respect for human rights. Each side exploited the uncertainty regarding Kosovo's future political status to "justify" their violent campaigns. Albanian extremists encouraged the notion that the Serbs might come back, since Yugoslavia's sovereignty over Kosovo remained intact in the resolution; therefore, it was vital to expel as many Serbs as possible, burn their homes, and make Kosovo "pure" of ethnic Serbs. This way the Serbs would have nothing to return to, strengthening Kosovo's claim for independence. Likewise, Serb extremists encouraged the remaining Serbs not to cooperate with UNMIK or KFOR, since Kosovo still belonged to Serbia and all decisions regarding local administration, public services, and security should still come from Belgrade. Those Serbs willing to cooperate with UNMIK and other international agencies arriving in Kosovo were often threatened or intimidated from cooperating by Serb hard-liners. This uncertainty over Kosovo's future stymied efforts to start dialogue and interaction between the two communities.

One major omission in Resolution 1244 was any mention of protecting minorities and promoting multiethnicity. Security Council members should have understood that the main human rights and security problem in Kosovo would be the treatment of the Serb, Roma, Turk, Muslim Slav, and other minorities. It would have helped if KFOR and UNMIK could have cited Security Council language and, more important, explicit commitment to a multiethnic Kosovo. Even UNMIK officials, at times baffled and frustrated by the relentless attacks on minorities, would say that Resolution 1244 doesn't say anything about a multiethnic Kosovo so maybe we should try for something else more realistic. This sent exactly the wrong signals to the extremists planning and carrying out the violence, especially Kosovo Albanians who because of their sheer numerical majority were now responsible for most of the abuses.

Resolution 1244 states that UNMIK should provide "transitional administration for the people of Kosovo" and "oversee the development of provisional democratic and self-governing institutions to ensure conditions for a peaceful and normal life for all inhabitants of Kosovo."[35] The international civilian presence would also provide basic administrative services for as long as necessary. The UN would then transfer administrative responsibility to local institutions whenever these were ready to function.

UNMIK also was charged with "maintaining law and order, including establishing local police forces and meanwhile through the deployment of international police personnel to serve in Kosovo" and with "protecting and promoting human rights."[36] Another key element of Resolution 1244 calls for UNMIK to ensure the "safe and unimpeded return of all refugees and displaced persons to their homes in Kosovo."[37]

The Security Council mandate also called for the demilitarization of the UCK and other armed Albanian groups and demanded that they "end immediately all offensive actions."[38] FRY forces also had to end immediately all violence and complete a "verifiable phased withdrawal from Kosovo of all military, police and paramilitary forces."[39]

Finally, Resolution 1244 encourages and "welcomes" the European Union's plan to develop and implement a "comprehensive approach to the economic development and stabilization of the region affected by the Kosovo crisis."[40]

Although the Security Council never used the word, what it had created was a modern trusteeship.[41] Other than for a brief period in Cambodia in the early 1990s, this was the first time in several decades that the UN had assumed responsibility for governing a territory. A few months later, the Security Council created another UN trusteeship in East Timor. The situation in East Timor, however, was clearer. The East Timorese had voted for independence and Indonesia had relinquished its claim to sovereignty. In Kosovo, however, the situation is much murkier; Serbia and the FRY insist that Kosovo belongs to them. In the meantime, the UN set up an interim administration in Kosovo with all the attributes of a UN protectorate, guarded by 40,000 NATO-led troops.

In May 2001 UNMIK unveiled a "constitutional framework" for Kosovo. While not deciding Kosovo's final status, it allows for significant self-rule in the meantime, including a 120-seat assembly with ten seats reserved for Serbs and ten seats for other minorities. The assembly will elect a president who will then name a prime minister who will form a government. Elections for the assembly were set for November 17, 2001. The final determination of Kosovo's political status was put off indefinitely. The decision not to hold a referendum on independence and UNMIK's refusal to call the document a constitution disappointed many Kosovo Albanians. UNMIK retains responsibility for justice and law enforcement and KFOR remains in charge of security. One expert analyst saw the plan as a "no confidence vote in Albanian leaders who have done little or nothing to stop the violence against Serbs and other minority populations in Kosovo."[42]

KOSOVO 1999: ONE OUTRAGE AMONG MANY

Most major international organizations wanted substantial roles in Kosovo. The story had been at the top of the news cycle for months, lots of money was suddenly available, and careers and reputations could be made working there. Plus, it was in Europe, which guaranteed ongoing media coverage and deep pockets among funders.

This attention to Kosovo raises further moral dilemmas. Kosovo Albanians suffered terribly under the Serb regime after autonomy was revoked in 1989, and the scenes of ethnic cleansing in early 1999 shocked world opinion. Humanitarian and human rights officials usually cringe when asked to "rank" suffering or make comparisons of horrors. But many quietly questioned the attention and especially the money and resources devoted to Kosovo compared to what arguably were situations of even greater horror and more desperate need in Sierra Leone, Angola, and Congo.

Defenders of the NATO intervention sometimes exaggerated casualty figures in Kosovo to rebut or preempt this criticism.[43] U.S. secretary of defense William Cohen had expressed alarm during the air campaign that 100,000 Kosovo Albanians were unaccounted for and stated that they may have been murdered. Others mentioned figures of 20,000 to 50,000 killed. The real number remains unknown and will probably never be known, but it is probably in the neighborhood of 5,000 to 10,000, which includes combatants on both sides and civilian Albanians, Serbs, Roma, and Muslim

Slavs who were killed or disappeared during the conflict. Exhumations completed by investigators from the International Criminal Tribunal for the Former Yugoslavia (ICTY) had uncovered 3,620 bodies by December 2000.[44] Tribunal spokesperson Paul Risley was not far off when he stated that "the final number of bodies uncovered will be less than 10,000, and probably more accurately determined as between two and three thousand."[45]

While I think it is obscene to engage in such arguments when the number killed is more than anyone can bear, this question has become politicized. Implicitly, and sometimes explicitly, higher numbers of casualties are used to "explain" or "understand" current attacks on non-Albanians and to show that whatever is happening now is not as bad as what came before.[46] For those who care about such counts, the gap is narrower than the supporters of the bombing would have one believe.

NOTES

1. Tito had granted Kosovo autonomous status in 1974.

2. The answer given by Serbian constitutionalists was that the Kosovo Albanians were not a "nation" but rather a "nationality." Their nation was Albania. Likewise for the Hungarians in the Vojvodina region of Serbia—they were a nationality only and not a nation. Their nation was Hungary. Milosevic also stripped autonomous status from Vojvodina in 1989. Under the Yugoslav constitutional system, only a nation could secede from the federation; thus Kosovo and Vojvodina cannot secede.

3. But the break was never complete and changed over time. According to Tim Judah, this was especially the case with the health care system, where many Albanian professionals continued to work and where people needing specialized care had no choice but to seek treatment in the state system. Judah, *Kosovo: War and Revenge* (New Haven: Yale University Press, 2000), p. 72.

4. Holbrooke's memoirs on Dayton include an episode where he and Milosevic are out for a walk and see a group of Kosovo Albanians at a fence holding up signs. Holbrooke suggests that they go over to talk to them and Milosevic immediately rejects the idea, insisting that Kosovo is an "internal" problem. Richard Holbrooke, *To End a War* (New York: Random House, 1998), p. 234.

5. For a fascinating and comprehensive account of the origins of the UCK, see Judah, *Kosovo: War and Revenge,* pp. 99–163, and Judah, "A History of the Kosovo Liberation Army," in William Joseph Buckley, ed., *Kosovo: Contending Voices on Balkan Interventions* (Grand Rapids, Mich.: Eerdmans Publishing, 2000), pp. 108–115.

6. Judah, *Kosovo: War and Revenge,* p. 117.

7. Ibid., p. 111.

8. Human Rights Watch, *Humanitarian Law Violations in Kosovo* (New York: Human Rights Watch 1998), pp. 28–32.

9. Michael MccGwire, "Why Did We Bomb Belgrade," *International Affairs* 76 (January 2000):5.

10. Agence France Presse, February 23, 1998.

11. Quoted in Dusko Doder and Louise Branson, *Milosevic: Portrait of a Tyrant* (New York: Free Press, 1999), p. 242.

12. Ibid., pp. 245–246.

13. OSCE, *Kosovo/Kosova: As Seen, As Told, part 1, An Analysis of the Human Rights Findings of the OSCE Kosovo Verification Mission October 1998 to June 1999* (Warsaw: OSCE, 1999), p. vii. This is the most authoritative and comprehensive account of human rights abuses during the most intense period of the conflict in Kosovo.

14. Ibid., pp. 149–158.

15. Ibid., p. 122.

16. See Human Rights Watch, *Kosovo: Rape as a Weapon of Ethnic Cleansing* (New York: Human Rights Watch, March 2000) for a detailed account of how Serb forces used rape as a systematic tool for ethnic cleansing.

17. *Kosovo/Kosova: As Seen, As Told,* part 1, p. 127.

18. The killing of forty-five Albanians on January 15, 1999, in Racak galvanized world opinion against the Serb regime. Among those killed were an eighteen-year-old woman and a twelve-year-old child. Some corpses had been decapitated. In the week leading up to the massacre, four Serb police had been ambushed and killed in the area, and the Serb forces greatly increased their presence prior to the assault on Racak. *See Kosovo/Kosova: As Seen, As Told,* part 1, pp. 353–355.

19. "It is more than possible, of course, that KLA tactics were not a miscalculation, but a deliberate strategy, designed to incite the Serbs to commit massacres that would eventually force NATO to intervene." Michael Ignatieff, *Virtual War: Kosovo and Beyond* (New York: Henry Holt, 2000), p. 58.

20. One KVM analyst noted, "KLA continued its provocations against the security forces with the rhetoric of fighting for liberty, but the substantive agenda may well be to trigger heavy responses from the Serb side that would invite a NATO reaction." KVM internal report, January 4–13, 1999.

21. CIA agents admitted providing training and equipment to the UCK and also giving them intelligence on Serb troop movements. See Tom Walker and Aidan Laverty, "CIA Aided Kosovo Guerrilla Army," *Sunday Times* (London), March 12, 2000. See also Steven Erlanger, "A One Time Ally Becomes a Problem, *New York Times*, March 25, 2001, Week in Review, p. 16.

22. General Wesley K. Clark, *Waging Modern War* (New York: Public Affairs, 2001), p. 335.

23. KVM internal report, February 23–March 11, 1999. The Independent International Commission on Kosovo led by former ICTY prosecutor Richard Goldstone was even more critical of the UCK, noting: "Serbia initially implemented the agreement and withdrew its forces accordingly. The KLA, by contrast, took advantage of the new situation and renewed military action. In fact, KLA forces moved in to take up positions vacated by the redeployed Serbian forces. The UN as well as NATO and the OSCE were alarmed by the KLA's actions. According to the UN Secretary-General, 'Recent attacks by Kosovo Albanian paramilitary units have indicated their readiness, capability and intention to actively pursue the advantage gained by the partial withdrawal of the police and military formations. . . . Reports of new weapons, ammunition and equipment indicate that the capacity of those units to crisply defend themselves is still fairly good. This development is disturbing.'" *The Kosovo Report*, International Independent Commission on Kosovo, available online at http://www.reliefweb.int/library/documents/thekosovoreport.htm

24. KVM internal report, January 18–23, 1999.

25. KVM internal report, March 3, 1999.

26. KVM internal report, March 5–12, 1999.

27. "Background Paper on Compliance with Rambouillet," KVM internal report, February 23–March 11, 1999, p. 4.

28. KVM internal report, February 7–20, 1999, p. 3.

29. KVM internal report, January 18–23, 1999, p. 2.

30. OSCE, *Kosovo/Kosova: As Seen, As Told,* part 1, p. 137.

31. Ironically, Kumanovo was the site of a great Serbian victory in the First Balkan War, of 1912–1913, resulting in Serbia reasserting its control over Kosovo.

32. General Wesley K. Clark, *Waging Modern War* (New York: Public Affairs 2001) p. 361.

33. KVM internal report, February 7–20, 1999.

34. And also confirms the territorial integrity of the "other States of the region, as set out in the Helsinki Final Act and annex 2." This reference was primarily to reassure Former Yugoslav Republic of Macedonia (FYROM), which has a substantial Albanian minority, that its territorial borders were not at risk. It also can be seen as a warning to Albania not even to think about any territorial expansion to create a "greater Albania."

35. UN Security Council Resolution 1244 (June 10, 1999), par. 10.

36. Ibid., par. 11(i, j).

37. Ibid., par. 11(k).

38. Ibid., par. 15.

39. Ibid., par. 3.

40. Ibid., par. 17.

41. In March 2001, the Working Group on the Legal Framework convened to draft recommendations on how Kosovo could achieve maximum self-governance without predetermining its final political status.

42. Tim Judah, "A Sensible Plan for Kosovo," *New York Times*, May 23, 2001.

43. Judah makes the point bluntly in discussing the growing demand for action in late 1998: "These massacres and executions were revolting but, in terms of numbers, compared to say those killed in Bosnia at the beginning of the war in 1992 or the thousands killed in Srebrenica in 1995, they were negligible. Likewise, Serbs were being kidnapped and murdered." Judah, *Kosovo: War and Revenge,* p. 180. Moreover, the number killed in Kosovo was less compared to those being killed contemporaneously in Sudan and Sierra Leone. The disparity in the international community's response to all these horrible situations became a major element in the debate over the "humanitarian intervention."

44. OSCE, Mission in Kosovo, Human Rights Division, "Missing Persons Section—Identification Project, Identification Statistics" (document of file with the author). Dozens of people have been reported to have gone missing since the end of the war in June 1999 and should not be included in the war-time casualty figures. Yet as discussed in Chapter 5, most, if not all, of the missing persons, regardless of when they disappeared, are probably dead.

45. Jonathan Steele, "West Exaggerated Killings by Serbs in Kosovo," *Guardian Weekly,* August 24–30, 2000, p. 4.

46. The debate is also important because it bears on the moral justification for going to war. The number of Albanian civilians killed by the Serbs before the war started is central to determining whether this was a "just war." The relatively low figure established by the ICTY's forensic scientists "does not make comfortable reading for NATO." See Bill McSweeney, "Virtual Reality: There's Nothing Virtual About Killing," *Irish Times,* March 11, 2000, reviewing Ignatieff's *Virtual War: Kosovo and Beyond.*

3

The UN Interim Administration Mission in Kosovo: An Unwieldy Beast

Frenzied discussions in New York, Washington, and Europe focused on who would get what piece of the Kosovo pie. Some resisted giving the UN much at all given its perceived failures in Bosnia. The OSCE lobbied hard to get most of the mandate, arguing that it was the primary security operation in Europe, that Kosovo was a European problem, and that the OSCE had done a good job elsewhere in the Balkans. NATO argued strenuously that it was happy to cooperate with whatever civilian administration emerged but that it would never come under its control. The model NATO cited was Bosnia, where the civilian administration had no authority over Implementation Force (IFOR) and later Stabilization Force (SFOR) troops.

One positive lesson learned from the Bosnia experience was to avoid having too many chiefs, and UN planners consciously decided not to recreate the Hydra-headed structure of Bosnia for Kosovo.[1] In Bosnia, on the civilian side, there is a high representative, but no one knows exactly whom this person represents. There is a special representative of the Secretary-General, a chief of mission of the OSCE, and a special envoy of the UN High Commissioner for Refugees (UNHCR). Added to this mix was the commander of IFOR/SFOR. It is no wonder that the people in Bosnia were confused. One UN official noted, "We looked at the civilian structure in Bosnia and said whatever happens, don't do that again in Kosovo."[2]

When the dust settled on the negotiations over Kosovo, a much more streamlined structure emerged. Four "pillars" of civilian activity would report to one person, the special representative of the Secretary-General (SRSG). KFOR would remain outside of the UNMIK structure and the commander would report to NATO headquarters in Belgium.

On the civilian side, the UNHCR became known as Pillar One. Headed by a deputy SRSG, UNHCR was responsible for coordinating and overseeing all humanitarian assistance programs in Kosovo. This was an enormous task since humanitarian assistance poured into Kosovo. Over 400 NGOs

37

were soon present—some known and established operations and others much less professional or competent—drawn by the lure of media exposure and the desire of many to help. UNHCR assigned some of its most able people to Kosovo in the start-up period; many had worked there before the conflict erupted and had also worked in the refugee camps in Macedonia and Albania. UNHCR logistics specialists arranged delivery of food, building materials, tools, seeds and fertilizers, medicine, stoves, and firewood.

UNHCR protection officers, along with the OSCE, also took the lead in identifying problems faced by minorities in Kosovo, many of whom were internally displaced. Along with the OSCE, UNHCR formed the Joint Task Force on Minorities in August 1999 and soon issued the first in a series of reports documenting attacks against minorities and the vulnerable position of most non-Albanians in Kosovo. This task force has played a central role in forging protection strategies and keeping the focus on the ongoing violence in Kosovo.

Pillar Two, Civil Administration, was assigned to the United Nations itself. The backbone of governance, Pillar Two is responsible for providing basic services to all Kosovars, which means that removing trash, registering births and deaths, repairing roads, providing utilities, getting the court system (including the prisons) up and running, issuing business licenses, and collecting taxes all fell to the United Nations. This was in many ways the most challenging set of tasks assigned to the international community. The UN has almost no experience in these fields and had few people with the expertise to perform any of the essential and basic government functions. A mad recruiting scramble ensued, with many well-intentioned but poorly qualified people arriving in a war-torn society where almost nothing worked. Also, about 800,000 people returned almost at once from exile and needed just about everything to restart their lives. Starting from scratch does not begin to describe the hurdles Pillar Two faced.

To make their work even more difficult, the UCK tried to take over running as much of Kosovo as they could. UCK soldiers and police (PU) assumed responsibility in many towns, installing themselves in mayors' offices and holding themselves out as the civilian authority. The UN's painfully slow recruitment and deployment of civilian personnel allowed the UCK structure to grow and fill the governance vacuum. As each day went by, the UCK parallel and wholly illegal structure became harder and harder to uproot, undermining efforts to create the rule of law and respect for human rights.

The OSCE occupied Pillar Three, focusing on institution building and monitoring and reporting on human rights. The OSCE is the lead player in organizing and holding elections. The OSCE had solid Balkan experience running similar operations in Bosnia-Herzegovina and Croatia. It had many people who had worked in the KVM who had continued working in refugee camps in Macedonia and Albania, and they quickly redeployed to Kosovo in June 1999. These people knew Kosovo very well from their KVM experience and were able to hit the ground running. OSCE also had much logistical equipment already in the region, especially vehicles, office equipment, computers, and communication systems. They also had one of the most important features of all: previously recruited and trained local employees (drivers, interpreters, and secretarial staff), who returned to work quickly and efficiently.

The OSCE created various divisions to carry out its mandate. A democratization unit worked on building the capacity of local political parties and NGOs. Women's participation and leadership of local groups became a special focus of the OSCE democratization unit's work.

The OSCE established a police school to train a new police force for Kosovo. This was a classic institution-building activity and the police school is one of the success stories of the international community's work in Kosovo.

The Rule of Law and Human Rights Department of the OSCE has about fifty international staff. The Rule of Law Division focuses on training judges and prosecutors and initially on monitoring judicial proceedings. It also worked on creating an ombudsperson's office, drafting new laws for Kosovo and reviewing existing laws to see if they complied with international human rights standards. The Rule of Law Division's work overlaps with Pillar Two's Department of Judicial Affairs. This duplication has had negative effects on the efforts to rebuild Kosovo's judiciary.

The Human Rights Division assumed primary responsibility for gathering, verifying, and reporting on human rights violations. Human rights field officers deployed to the OSCE's five regional centers (Pristina, Prizren, Pec, Mitrovica, and Gnjilane) and to smaller field offices throughout Kosovo. They travel frequently in their areas of responsibility, interviewing victims and witnesses of violations and submitting weekly reports to the headquarters staff in Pristina. These reports provide crucial information to UNMIK and sometimes to the international press. UNHCR and OSCE/Human Rights were the first to document the violence in Kosovo directed first and foremost against the minority communities and later against Albanians, and this information was a core part of the periodic reports issued by the Joint Task Force on Minorities. The OSCE Human Rights Division was one of the first to discern patterns in this violence, suggesting that it was organized and systematic and frequently involved UCK leaders and fighters.

Initially, the Office of the UN High Commissioner for Human Rights (UNHCHR) lobbied hard to be the primary actor in all human rights activities. The UNHCHR had opened a small office in Pristina before the NATO air campaign and had an office in Belgrade mandated to cover all the FRY.

The UNHCHR, however, has difficulty mounting field operations, and a limited budget and personnel shortages hindered a quick and massive deployment, which was precisely what Kosovo required. It lost out to the OSCE but maintains an office in Pristina, outside UNMIK's structure; this gives the UNHCHR some flexibility and freedom to work on several issues and opportunities that are more problematic for UNMIK—for example, the question of the Kosovo Albanians detained in Serbia proper.

The European Union (EU) constitutes Pillar Four. This pillar works on economic reconstruction. While Kosovo did not suffer the brunt of NATO's bombing, the Serb government had consistently scrimped when it came to investing in Kosovo; there was little industry, a growing population, and few natural resources. Kosovo was by far the poorest part of the FRY. Moreover, the Serb forces had wreaked destruction in Kosovo as they departed, especially in western Kosovo (Pec and Djakovica) and in Vucitrn and Podujevo. Thousands of houses were burned, fields heavily landmined, and livestock killed or stolen.

Even among its supporters the EU is known as slow, ponderous, and bureaucratic; and that is true even for run-of-the-mill project approval in Brussels. For working in an emergency situation requiring flexibility and lots of room for initiative, the EU was a bad fit for Kosovo, especially in the early days. Slow to deploy, with funding always in the pipeline but rarely available, Pillar Four was the target of frequent criticism. Its emphasis on macroeconomics and revenue raising might be appropriate in a more settled situation, but not in Kosovo.

THE SPECIAL REPRESENTATIVE
OF THE SECRETARY-GENERAL'S OFFICE

Heading all four pillars is the SRSG. Acting SRSG Sergio Vieira de Mello arrived in Kosovo shortly after NATO troops in mid-June. About six weeks later, Bernard Kouchner arrived to take over from de Mello. Kouchner was one of the founders of Médecins Sans Frontières (Doctors Without Borders) and had recently served as minister of health in the French government. A Dane, former defense minister Hans Haekkerup, succeeded Kouchner in January 2001.

A principal deputy SRSG, along with the four heads of pillars, formed the SRSG's executive committee. They meet each morning with the goal of establishing a coordinated approach across UNMIK's vast mandate.[3]

Kouchner had a small team of political advisers, some of whom had participated in the Rambouillet negotiations in February and March 1999. Once this team started, the UN's Department of Political Affairs (DPA) was largely sidelined. This had important consequences on the quality of political advice given to the SRSG and on the human rights situation. DPA had several people who had followed the situation in Kosovo for years and knew not only the key local players but also their relative strengths and their degree of support within Kosovo society. Most importantly, DPA officials had a healthy skepticism of the UCK and its commitment to human rights and the rule of law. Yet the SRSG and his team in Pristina forged their own policy without consulting New York, who were reduced to reviewing and commenting on positions that had already been decided and even publicized in Kosovo. This is a structural problem within the United Nations: how can peacekeeping operations incorporate better the often extensive expertise and contacts of DPA officials who have followed a country for years?

The SRSG has a press office headed by a spokesperson, a strategic planning unit, a gender adviser, and a human rights adviser. A Legal Affairs Department, composed mostly of seconded staff from UN headquarters, provides legal advice and drafts regulations that become part of the binding law of Kosovo under the UN administration.

CIVPOL: THE UNMIK POLICE

An increasingly frequent component of modern complex peacekeeping operations is CIVPOL. Kosovo has the largest authorized CIVPOL force ever: 4,800. CIVPOL in Kosovo have primary policing authority, meaning they are armed and have the power to arrest and detain.[4] The head of CIVPOL, Commissioner Christopher Albiston of the Royal Ulster Constabulary, reports to the SRSG; CIVPOL is not part of KFOR. The myriad challenges facing CIVPOL and the international civilian police officers' interactions with OSCE human rights officers, KFOR, and the new Kosovo Police Service is discussed in Chapter 7.

NOTES

1. Interview with UN official, New York, November 8, 2000.
2. Interview with UN official, New York, February 23, 2001.
3. UNHCR, the head of Pillar One (Humanitarian Assistance), ceased being a pillar in July 2000 and reverted to being a regular UNHCR presence in Kosovo. In May 2001 a new Pillar One was created, covering law enforcement and the judiciary.
4. This is unique power shared only by CIVPOL in East Timor. Most UN CIVPOL operations monitor only and do not have the power to arrest; most are not usually armed. This was true in Rwanda and is the case in Bosnia, Angola, and Sierra Leone.

4

The NATO Kosovo Force

The NATO Kosovo Force (KFOR) is wholly outside UNMIK's structure; a major challenge for both is to ensure close communication, cooperation, and collaboration. It is somewhat misleading, however, to talk about KFOR as if it were one, cohesive force. Unfortunately, it is not.

KFOR divides Kosovo into five regions, each commanded by a major NATO troop contributor.[1] Overall command of all KFOR troops is in the hands of the Commander KFOR, a position that changes every six months. The first KFOR commander was Major General Sir Mike Jackson, a British officer who was involved in the negotiations with the Federal Yugoslav Army at Kumanovo, Macedonia, that ended the NATO air campaign. General Jackson, as all subsequent KFOR commanders, in turn reported to NATO headquarters in Belgium and to the Supreme Allied Commander, who in June 1999 was U.S. general Wesley Clark.

The KFOR commanders always preach unity and how KFOR is truly one seamless web. However, this has never been true. Major contingent commanders check with commanding officers back in their national capitals and then inform Commander KFOR if they can or will follow his orders. For example, after violence flared in the divided city of Mitrovica in early February 2000, the Pentagon ordered the U.S. general in charge of the U.S. contingent in Kosovo not to allow his troops to be deployed there. Serb demonstrators had thrown rocks and snowballs at U.S. troops who had come from their sector in eastern Kosovo to reinforce the French contingent. The Pentagon deemed the risk to U.S. soldiers too high given U.S. politicians' zero tolerance for armed professionals to suffer casualties. So General Klaus Reinhardt, the German commander of KFOR at the time, was forced to find troops from other contingents to deal with the tense situation in Mitrovica.[2]

KFOR entered a smoldering Kosovo on June 12, 1999. Departing Serb forces conducted a scorched earth campaign on their routes out of Kosovo.

KFOR guarding a church in Kosovo Polje/Fushe Kosov.

Houses burned and looting was widespread. NATO bombs had also caused some destruction.

A different kind of smoldering, but one more difficult to control and extinguish, was firing a desire for revenge among some Albanians. Those who had stayed had suffered greatly from the Serb forces' depredations. Many had lived in their houses and apartments for weeks at a time without being able to venture forth; 800,000 others streamed back from the camps in Albania and Macedonia within days. What they saw was often gut-wrenching: houses and buildings burned and looted, farms empty of live-stock and seed, businesses destroyed. Towns such as Malisevo, a well-known center of UCK activity and support, suffered severe damage. Vucitrn, near Mitrovica in northern Kosovo, was a string of skeletal struc-tures, often with only the chimney and outer wall left standing.

Some KFOR troops were unwilling to stop the revenge attacks. Some did not understand that their previous mission, to protect Kosovo Albanians from the Serb forces, was now obsolete. The new mission quickly had become how to protect Kosovo's minorities from attacks by some Albanians. Other KFOR troops had been ordered not to stop the violence. For example, as Albanians returned to Vucitrn in June, they quickly started to loot and burn Serb houses and the Serbian Orthodox church and monastery. Roma, who were subject to a collective presumption of guilt for having collaborated with Serbs, also had to flee, and their houses were burned. French KFOR troops, standing outside a burning Roma house in Vucitrn, when asked by a reporter why they did not seem to be fulfilling their mission of "reassuring the local population" when it came to the Serbs and Roma, responded, "The orders are to let them pillage." When told this was crazy, one soldier responded, "Of course it's mad, but those are our orders."[3]

KFOR IN MITROVICA

French KFOR troops' action up the road from Vucitrn in Mitrovica in the early days of the NATO occupation also had lasting and negative consequences. The Ibar River runs right through the northern Kosovo city of Mitrovica. Before the war, Serbs and Albanians lived on both sides of the river, but the Serbs tended to live in the north. As the Serb forces fled north out of Kosovo to Serbia proper, many Serb and Roma civilians followed them. Albanians too were already on the move trying to return to their homes all over Kosovo. French KFOR, for reasons that are still not understood, stopped at the Ibar River and erected a checkpoint.[4] Albanians were not allowed to cross into northern Mitrovica or indeed into northern Kosovo. In effect, the French had partitioned Mitrovica, which became a divided city like Mostar in Bosnia.

This enraged the Albanians, and rightly so. Albanians were prohibited from reclaiming their homes in the north. While some Albanians who had never left northern Mitrovica remained, the north became predominantly Serb, whereas southern Mitrovica was overwhelmingly Albanian; only a handful of elderly Serbs remained near the Orthodox church in the south. The bridge across the Ibar River became the proverbial flashpoint for demonstrations. In August 1999, rockets were fired from the south and hit Serb apartments along the northern riverbank. Albanians would walk to the bridge and gaze over the barbed wire and across the river where they could see their old apartments, now occupied by Serbs who in turn had been forced to leave their apartments in the south.

The French KFOR action sealed off all of northern Kosovo from the rest, creating the largest Serb sector with a direct land border to Serbia proper that had no substantial Albanian population in between. The French troops' actions poisoned an already suspicious relationship with the Albanians, who assumed—with some history on their side—that the French were pro-Serb. Also, the important Trpca mining complex now lay in Serb hands. Trpca is by far the most important economic asset in Kosovo, although some experts question its real value given depleted reserves and antiquated equipment. Nevertheless, it is a potent economic symbol for Kosovo, and the Albanians insist it belongs to all in Kosovo. French KFOR have had a very tense relationship with the Albanian community in Mitrovica and environs from the earliest days.

The de facto border between the Serb-dominated north and the rest of Kosovo created fissures in important institutions and reinforced the ethnic divide. For example, the main hospital in the region is in northern Mitrovica. After a few months of tense but relatively peaceful coexistence in the hospital, relations broke down in October 1999. Albanian hospital personnel, who had been bused in from the south each day, demanded that they be treated as professionals and not be forced to get their pay on the street. Serb extremists in the north exploited this rift and started to organize crowds who would chant insults at the bus each day and sometimes throw rocks. After hurried negotiations that failed, the Albanians pulled out of the hospital; Albanian patients had to be taken to facilities in the south. Serb extremists encouraged the split, happy to have complete control of the hospital. Yet moderates on both sides regretted the action; some Serb doctors said they wanted to continue working with their Albanian colleagues but that this was no longer possible.

A similar breakdown occurred in the university, which was also located in the north; it soon became a wholly Serb facility. Serb leaders in Mitrovica said Albanians could return to the campus when Serbs would be able to return to the university in Pristina, which had become entirely Albanian. This was cynical in the extreme, because the Serbs knew that no Serb could go to the university in Pristina without risking his or her life.

KFOR AND THE VIOLENCE AGAINST MINORITIES

KFOR got off to a slow start in protecting minorities. KFOR's initial policy was to be soft on revenge attacks. U.S. military and diplomatic staff especially were quick to explain and even excuse the attacks on minorities. Their position was that after such violence and ethnic cleansing, vengeance happens. Secretary of State Madeleine Albright contributed to this attitude when she commented after the massacre of fourteen Serb farmers in July 1999, "Here was obviously a dreadful incident. We can't forget that there were some pretty disgusting things that took place before, but the system is set up in order to protect them. They should stay."[5] General Wesley Clark, who was in charge of the NATO air campaign, said in August 1999, "I am not going to point fingers at the KLA. The KLA leadership has been very cooperative with us at the top level."[6] Clark maintained that violence seemed "spontaneous" or linked to organized crime. Yet even in early August, clear evidence of KLA/UCK responsibility for much of the violence in Kosovo was emerging.

A prevailing and widespread perception in Kosovo was that Thaci,

Agim Ceku (former military commander of the UCK), UCK zone commander Ramush Haradinaj, and other major UCK leaders had the full backing and support of the United States. This stemmed from the alleged close
relationship between James Rubin, Albright's spokesman and a key adviser
to the secretary of state, and UCK leaders. A UN official notes, "The
Americans told us that we must deal with Thaci and Ceku, that these are
'our boys' and to forget about Rugova because he is a drunk."[7] UNMIK,
KFOR, and other major international players reinforced this perception by
constantly meeting with and calling on Thaci and Ceku, reinforcing the
notion that they were indispensable interlocutors. This was a big mistake in
the view of many informed Albanian observers, who insist that able and
popular moderates were thus overlooked and sidelined. For example, religious leaders from the various faiths in Kosovo had maintained communication even during the bombing and were in the vanguard of promoting
interethnic dialogue. Yet they were largely ignored by UNMIK except for
periodic visits to Gracanica to discuss concerns relating to the Serb minority with Bishop Artemije.[8] While it was necessary to talk to the UCK, it was
not sufficient since they were not representative of the broader Kosovo
Albanian society.

Another reason was fear that the UCK was dangerous and could harm
NATO. The UCK had served as NATO's surrogate ground troops in the war
because NATO states had limited their intervention to an air campaign.
Thus some kind of debt was owed the UCK in the mind of some Western
leaders. This had the unintended consequence of inflating the UCK's estimate of their role in the war. Some UCK leaders really believe that they
won the war with just a little help from NATO.[9] This delusion had serious
consequences that will be explored later, but UCK commanders felt that
they had earned the right to rule Kosovo and also the right to brutally treat
remaining ethnic minorities. Both KFOR and UNMIK were much too slow
in disabusing the UCK of this view and in reining them in.

One leading Kosovo Albanian analyst criticizes KFOR and UNMIK
for their soft approach in the early days, noting that this enabled the
extremist element in the UCK to take control of numerous sectors of the
economy and to intimidate moderates. "Instead of cracking down on the
warlords, KFOR and UNMIK allowed them to divide Kosovo into different
zones where these warlords generate enormous wealth."[10] One UN
CIVPOL officer serving in Lipljan noted early on, "We sat around too
much, we should all have been much more pro-active from the start. We
came to help and protect people and now we have all these dead bodies."

If the "possibility of revenge increases the desire," then KFOR and
UNMIK should have made it clear to the UCK leaders that revenge and
violence would not be tolerated in internationally administered Kosovo.[11]
Another Kosovo Albanian analyst maintains that most people would have

supported a stricter KFOR policy; after all, "the Albanians were cheering NATO and thanking them for liberating Kosovo from the Serbs. They knew it was NATO and not the UCK that had defeated the Serb forces."[12] An Albanian noted, "The UCK are showing off now, claiming credit for something they didn't do and people don't like it."

The UCK quickly stepped into the security and political vacuum created by the hasty departure of the Serb forces and the Serb regime, creating the fundamental "facts on the ground" for the lawlessness that continues to plague Kosovo. Parallel structures dominated by UCK or handpicked UCK operatives soon ran many cities and municipalities, imposing taxes and usurping prime businesses and housing. Some UCK "talked openly of their 'zero tolerance' policy, which means that they will allow no Serbs to remain in their areas."[13]

Many Albanians I interviewed shared the view that if KFOR and UNMIK had acted with greater toughness, rigor, and clarity in the early days, violence would have diminished and many problems relating to security, economic development, and relations between the ethnic communities would also have been less grave. One insisted that the international community should have stated on June 12, 1999, that they "are here to deal with all Kosovars, there will be no more ethnic labels, you are all here, we won't let you exploit ethnic grievances or divisions. We won't let you use or misuse past abuses for economic and political gain now. This is hypocrisy."[14] These are strong words, but one reason why KFOR and UNMIK were slow to crack down hard on the new violators of human rights was because some had recently been the victims of abuses seen on television screens around the world.

NOTES

1. The five regions and their commands are Multinational Brigade Center (MNB), United Kingdom; MNB North, France; MNB South, Germany; MNB East, United States; MNB West, Italy.

2. Steven Erlanger, "NATO General Hopes G.I.'s Will Return to Kosovo Town," *New York Times,* February 28, 2000.

3. Tim Judah, *Kosovo: War and Revenge* (New Haven: Yale University Press, 2000), p. x.

4. Interview with U.S. military official, Washington, D.C., April 2000. Another account has Sergio Vieira de Mello, acting SRSG at the time, deciding not to let Albanians cross into the north. Antoine Garapon and Olivier Mongin, "Les Alliés doivent reprendre l'initiative," *Le Monde,* March 25, 2000 p. xi.

5. Secretary Albright, KFOR Commander General Jackson, and SRSG Kouchner, cited in Benjamin Ward, "The Failure to Protect Minorities in Post-War Kosovo," *Helsinki Monitor 2000,* July 29, 2000, p. 35.

6. "Clark Sees No Evidence KLA Behind Attacks On Serbs," Reuters, August 13, 1999. Yet Clark in his memoirs describes a very different approach

toward hard-liners in Bosnia after the conflict there. Clark notes that his policy was for NATO troops to discredit the Bosnian Serb hard-liners using several tactics, including supporting Serb moderates, thus splitting and weakening those opposing the Dayton Accords. Gen. Wesley K. Clark, *Waging Modern War* (New York: Public Affairs, 2001), p. 84. One wishes that Clark and other KFOR and UNMIK leaders had implemented a similar strategy in Kosovo in 1999.

7. Interview, New York, February 27, 2001.

8. *See* International Crisis Group, *Religion in Kosovo,* available at www.crisisweb.org/projects/showreport.cfm?reportid=226, January 31, 2001. The ICG recommends that UNMIK create greater support for interfaith dialogue and give it greater standing.

9. While some UCK troops fought courageously, the extent and impact of their fighting is debatable. They rarely held territory for very long; they ambushed Serb police and military patrols and conducted a typical insurgency campaign, usually operating in small, mobile groups. The damage they inflicted on the Serb fighting machine, however, seems minimal. At the scene of one reportedly large and decisive battle on Mount Pastrik near the Albanian border, NATO investigators found after the war no evidence of heavy casualties. In fact, NATO was surprised by how little damage had been done to the Yugoslav Serb army, which they believe could have held out for quite some time. Judah, *Kosovo: War and Revenge,* p. 284. "Clark's targeteers are skeptical of KLA claims. The Albanian fighters exaggerated their own military impact." Michael Ignatieff, *Virtual War: Kosovo and Beyond* (New York: Henry Holt, 2000), p. 106. This is also an indictment of the NATO bombing, which caused much less damage to the Serb forces than the wartime press offensive would have had one believe.

10. Interview, Pristina, September 2000.

11. Serb analyst Aleksa Djilas, paraphrasing Stendhal, as quoted by Judah, *Kosovo: War and Revenge,* p. 312.

12. Interview, Pristina, September 2000.

13. Tim Judah, "A History of the Kosovo Liberation Army," in William J. Buckley, ed., *Kosovo: Contending Voices on Balkan Interventions* (Grand Rapids, Mich.: Eerdmans Publishing, 2000), p. 115.

14. Interview, Pristina, September 2000.

5

Human Rights in Kosovo

THE MORAL DILEMMAS

One risks sounding callous and hard-hearted in raising human rights abuses committed by some Albanians against Serbs, Roma, Turks, and Muslim Slavs in Kosovo following KFOR's entry in June 1999. Surely, some said, you can understand how the Albanians must have felt to come back to find houses destroyed, lives disrupted, relatives dead or missing, women raped, and children traumatized by witnessing unspeakable atrocities. All this is true, and many working with UNMIK and KFOR tried to understand, as much as possible without having endured the same awful experiences, what must have been going through the minds of the returning Kosovo Albanians.

The desire for revenge is human. Symbols of Serb dominance and culture quickly came under attack. Serb churches and monasteries all over Kosovo, the most visible signs of Serb rule, were looted and destroyed until KFOR troops started to put twenty-four-hour guards in front of those churches not yet demolished. Police stations and military bases not hit by NATO bombs also were quickly targeted and destroyed.

Attacks on individuals and their houses and businesses were more morally complex and problematic. While deplorable, violence against Serbs, Roma, Turks, and Muslim Slavs who had been members of the Serb police or military or who had helped the Serb forces in some way was "understandable." It would have been preferable to arrest and detain such people and then try them in a court of law for any crimes or violations of human rights or humanitarian law. But summary justice is common in the immediate aftermath of conflicts. Many of us had worked in Rwanda, Cambodia, Bosnia, Haiti, and similar places where revenge attacks against members of the previous regime occurred after a change in power.[1]

Also understandable was the desire to settle scores with those who had

A mosque and an Orthodox church in Prizren.

not directly participated in atrocities but who had profited from them by appropriating property or goods belonging to Albanians forced to abandon their homes and possessions. Others, especially some Roma, had allegedly assisted Serb forces by pointing out where Albanians were hiding and had dug graves in which Albanians killed by the Serb forces were buried. The Roma, who often were grave diggers in Kosovo, and who are traditionally discriminated against throughout Europe, now face even greater enmity because they have been branded as collaborators.

Many in UNMIK expected the desire for revenge to last for a while given the extent of the suffering inflicted on the Kosovo Albanians for at least the last ten years. But few were prepared for the ferocity of the violence that has endured for more than two years now. UNMIK head, SRSG Bernard Kouchner, expressed it well: "Here I discovered hatred deeper than anywhere in the world, more than in Cambodia or Vietnam or Bosnia."[2] Another disturbing feature was that many, but by no means all, Albanians had adopted a presumption of collective guilt concerning all Serbs and Roma. The "presumption of innocence" has a limited application in Kosovo. "There were few Serbs here, but all of them were more or less implicated in their dirty war," says one young man in Djakovica.[3] This rationale holds that if they are Serb or Roma, they are guilty of something, just by the mere fact of their ethnicity. Therefore, any violence against them is justified. This is a big challenge for KFOR and UNMIK: how to con-

vince many Albanians that not all Serbs or Roma are responsible for human
rights violations. Those who are must be punished, while those who are not
must be allowed to live peacefully wherever they want in Kosovo.

It was little use to argue that those most responsible for planning and
implementing the ethnic cleansing and other abuses had long ago left
Kosovo and were now ensconced in Belgrade. Any "big fish" had surely
fled Kosovo knowing full well that to remain meant almost certain death.
No matter, certain leaders of the Kosovo Albanian community stoked the
fires of hatred and promoted vengeance regardless how harmless or innocent the victim at hand.

This revenge cannot be accepted or understood just because what the
Serbs did was worse. The Albanians have no right to wreak vengeance,
even if it is on a lesser scale or does not have the formal backing of a state.
Former secretary of state Albright misses the point when she dismissed
ongoing violence against minorities in March 2000 by noting, "After all
that has happened, we do not expect rival communities in Kosovo to immediately join hands and start singing folk songs."[4]

Some analysts make a distinction without a difference between the
organized campaign by Serb regular and irregular forces and the ensuing
reprisals by Albanian extremists, who are also organized and for at least the
first eight months following NATO's entry constituted a "state" in everything but name. For example, journalist Sebastian Junger claims the Serbs
committed war crimes whereas the Albanians' actions are "just violence."[5]
Junger creates moral and legal confusion by ignoring the premeditated,
widespread, and systematic nature of the attacks on Serbs, other minorities,
and moderate Albanians since June 1999. These abuses fully meet any defi-
nition of war crimes or crimes against humanity. The only significant difference is one of scale—a difference of degree, not of kind—and that is
largely due to the presence of 40,000 KFOR troops and 4,000 international
police.[6]

The chief prosecutor for the International Criminal Tribunal for the
Former Yugoslavia, Carla del Ponte, has shown that she concurs with this
assessment. In November 2000, she asked the Security Council to amend
the tribunal's statute to cover crimes against humanity committed against
Serbs and other non-Albanians since NATO forces arrived in June 1999.[7]
Del Ponte recognized that what has happened in Kosovo since NATO and
UNMIK assumed responsibility is not a "different kind of killing." She said
the tribunal's "forced inaction over what has happened in Kosovo since
June 1999 . . . undermines the Tribunal's historical credibility. We must
ensure that the Tribunal's unique chance to bring justice to the populations
of the former Yugoslavia does not pass into history as having been flawed
and biased in favor of one ethnic group against another." Arguing that
extending the court's mandate is morally justified, del Ponte also noted that

such an extension could deter the "on-going ethnic cleansing campaign in Kosovo."

Few doubt that if KFOR troops left Kosovo, all the remaining Serbs or Roma would either have to flee or would be killed. For example, four Roma men, with help from UNHCR, returned to their burned-out homes in central Kosovo eighteen months after fleeing and seeking refuge in a Serb enclave protected by KFOR. They were murdered within forty-eight hours of returning to their homes; they had declined KFOR protection because they said their neighbors had insisted that they would be safe.[8] We need to recognize this violence for what it is: reverse ethnic cleansing, and one that is in no way justified or excusable because it is a response to an earlier attempt to "cleanse" Albanians from Kosovo. And most Albanians, to their great credit, abhor this violence, want it to stop, and for many months were too afraid to provide information to KFOR and the international police; but that is slowly changing.

The international community, however ill defined and amorphous, did not intervene in Kosovo and conduct what some have called the first "humanitarian war" to then preside over an orgy of violence and human rights violations by some of the very people rescued.[9]

The failure of the Serbian leadership in Belgrade to admit that its forces had committed atrocities in Kosovo complicates the moral land-scape. Albanians correctly pointed out that their willingness to begin any dialogue with Serbs would increase if Serbs recognized the horrors com-mitted in their name and apologized. Milosevic and other leaders, however, asserted that they had done nothing wrong and had nothing to apologize for, that "tragedies" occur in wars and that both sides suffered. This false moral equivalency plus a refusal to acknowledge war crimes by the Serbs made it more difficult for moderates in both the Albanian and Serbian com-munities in Kosovo to begin reconciliation. The Serb leadership would be wise to adopt the admonition of Rabbi Abraham Heschel, who stated that "some are guilty; all are responsible."[10] The extremists in both camps, how-ever, do not make such refined moral distinctions. They actually benefited from their intransigent views since they had no interest in a real multiethnic Kosovo. But the blame here falls overwhelmingly on the shoulders of the Serbian political leadership in Belgrade and on Serb extremists in Mitrovica.

A few Serb leaders in Kosovo have made halting efforts to apologize. Bishop Artemije, the head of the Serbian Orthodox Church in Kosovo, issued several statements in late 1999 and the beginning of 2000 expressing pain at the suffering inflicted on the Albanians. His assistant and spokesperson, Father Sava Janjic, fluent in English and experienced in dealing with the Western media, also issued several conciliatory statements expressing regret and sorrow for Serbian actions from the headquarters of the Serbian Orthodox Church located in the fourteenth-century monastery in Gracanica, 10 miles outside Pristina. President Vojislav Kostunica acknowledged Serb responsibility for atrocities during the wars in Croatia, Bosnia, and Kosovo and even hinted at an apology. While this was a huge improvement over Milosevic's intransigence, it did not satisfy most Albanians in Kosovo. No statement so far, however, is an unequivocal apology for the killings, rape, and ethnic cleansing and has thus failed to meet the Albanians' understandable and justified need.[11]

THE TABLES HAVE TURNED

The violence began immediately, with the first wave of arriving KFOR soldiers and returning refugees. Reports of Serbs being killed and Roma being rounded up, beaten, and tortured pepper the accounts of both KFOR troops and journalists on the scene those first few days. While deplorable, these acts largely were spasms of violence, unleashed at the sight of a smoking pile of rubble where once had been a house. Worse still was discovering that a loved one or friend had been killed or was missing. In these early weeks, KFOR and early-arriving UNMIK officials, though taken aback by the intensity of the hatred and violence, strained to understand what was driving the violence. Condemnations of the violence were usually qualified, couched in terms that softened the criticism by putting the abuses in "context."

In some areas, more destruction occurred following the NATO air campaign than during the bombing. Gnjilane, for example, was a largely Serb city in southeastern Kosovo. Serb forces did not destroy many houses in the town and there was not much violence compared to other parts of Kosovo. Once the Serb forces retreated, however, Gnjilane became a deadly place if you were Serb or Roma. Houses burned, people "disappeared," and looting of Serb-owned businesses was extensive. One of the worst incidents of violence occurred in a village near Gnjilane on July 23, 1999. Fourteen Serb males who were out tending their fields were murdered in broad daylight.

Similarly in Prizren, which suffered little damage during the war, the sight of burning houses was a familiar one from June to December 1999. On my first visit in mid-September 1999, I saw at least a dozen plumes of smoke circling into the sky from different parts of the city. These were Serb houses that had been torched by Albanian extremists. Many more houses burned after the NATO bombing than before in Prizren.

Overview of Minorities in Kosovo

Serbs and Roma in the major towns and cities quickly retreated either to enclaves in those towns or to northern Mitrovica and the three municipalities in the north where Serbs constitute a majority of the population.[12] Many left for Serbia proper. Out of an estimated 250,000 Serbs in prewar Kosovo, the number dropped steadily over the first year of NATO/UN occupation. UNHCR estimated that by the end of 2000 there were about 100,000 Serbs left in Kosovo.

The exact number of Roma in Kosovo has always been fuzzy. Moreover, the Roma themselves disagree on who is and is not a Roma. The population falls into three groups: Roma, Egyptians, and Ashkalia. Ashkalia tend to speak Albanian and often try to identify with the Albanian community; some reject being grouped with the Roma. Roma usually speak Serbian, although some speak Albanian also. Egyptians fall in between and maintain that they arrived in the Balkans from Egypt many years ago. The majority of all groups are physically distinguishable from Albanians, Serbs, and Slavs, and intermarriage is extremely rare. When asked, most Albanians will say that they do not distinguish among the three, that all are "gypsies" as far as they are concerned, and all indeed have been targeted in the aftermath of the NATO bombing.[13] In fact, one leading Albanian warned the Ashkalia not to go too far in trying to identify themselves as Albanians because Albanians would view this as an insult.

Albanians torched many Roma neighborhoods, especially in southern Mitrovica. The Roma fled to self-contained enclaves, often near Serbs, thereby reinforcing the notion that they were "collaborators" with the previous regime. Many have had to live in camps hastily erected by UNHCR. Despite UNHCR's best efforts, these camps are miserable places, often muddy or dusty depending on the season; people lived in overcrowded tents and there was virtually 100 percent unemployment. Whether in enclaves or camps, the Roma require twenty-four-hour protection by KFOR. About 30,000 Roma remained in Kosovo by the end of 2000; an unknown number had fled to Serbia proper, Macedonia, and elsewhere.

The Turks and Muslim Slavs have fared slightly better. Although most Albanians are Muslim, their religious ties with Turks and Muslim Slavs are very weak; ethnicity trumps religion in Kosovo. The Turks are concentrated in Prizren and a few outlying villages; Turkish communities also exist in Kosovo's other major cities. The Turks have kept a low profile since the bombing ended; they are subject to threats, harassment, and discrimination.

The Muslim Slavs live in most large cities, especially Prizren, and in several villages near Pec in the west. Preferring to call themselves "Bosniaks," the Muslim Slavs speak "Bosnian" or Serbo-Croatian. The Bosniak label is a form of self-preservation to distinguish themselves from Serbs. The problem is that their language, no matter what they call it, sounds like Serbian, which can literally be a death sentence if spoken in the wrong place at the wrong time. Many Bosniaks have "disappeared" since the bombing; some have been killed and many of their houses burned.

The Gorani are a Slavic people speaking their own form of Serbo-Croatian. They live mostly in the deep south of Kosovo, in the salient that stretches down to the Macedonian border. Largely Muslim, they once predominated in the municipality of Dragash. Albanian hard-liners have lashed out at the Gorani especially hard. Numerous cases of killings, disappearances, and beatings have occurred during the latter part of 1999 and throughout 2000. Grenades thrown into Gorani houses in Dragash seem to be a popular tactic to intimidate the Gorani into leaving. On September 21 and 30, 2000, several explosions occurred in Dragash, and Gorani homes were the targets. On March 6, 2001, a grenade exploded at a Gorani apartment in Dragash that had previously been targeted, seriously injuring one person and wounding two others, including an infant.[14] UNHCR estimates that at least half the original population of 30,000 Gorani had left Kosovo by the end of 2000.

There are also Kosovo Albanian Catholics. Living largely in the west near Pec and Djakovica, they reject the minority label and insist on their close ties with the rest of the Albanian population. However, Albanian Catholics have had difficulties in postwar Kosovo. Some Catholic villages in the west escaped relatively unscathed from the Serbs' depredations while neighboring villages were decimated. Some UCK leaders suspected the Catholics of having collaborated with the Serbs; this could be the reason why their villages were not touched. Some Catholic men were rounded up by UCK members and taken to their police stations for "informative talks." These sessions usually involved beatings and threats. Some of the men were kept for weeks; at least one has never returned home. In addition, Catholic cemeteries in Prizren and other towns have been vandalized. Albanian Protestants in Pec and Djakovica have also suffered harassment and threats.

The Detainees in Serbia Proper and the Missing

The detainees in Serbia and the missing, as much as any other issue from the conflict, continue to poison relations between the Serbian and Albanian communities. As the NATO campaign ended, Serb forces withdrew from Kosovo and took with them about 2,000 Albanian prisoners. The Serb forces put them in prisons in Serbia proper. About 2,800 other Albanians remain unaccounted for. As for the Serbs, those taken by the UCK are presumed dead. President Kostunica has made clarifying the fate of the missing Serbs a top priority, while the Albanians insist that releasing the Albanian detainees and discovering the fate of their missing must occur before any dialogue with Belgrade can take place.

The understandable emotional reaction to the missing and detainees issue, which grew directly from the nature of the conflict in 1998–1999, has had an ongoing and harmful impact on protecting human rights and promoting even the most modest form of interethnic understanding. "There will never be peace in Kosovo, there will never be peace in Serbia, and the world will never be in peace, if our children are not found and returned home," said Aferdeze Efendia, who speaks for many Albanians and whose own twenty-two-year-old son was taken away by Yugoslav police in 1999.[15]

Realizing this was a major issue, the Kosovo Transition Council (KTC), which was for a time the only quasi-governmental body that included Kosovars, established the Commission on the Detainees and the Missing in September 1999. Chaired by the UNHCHR head of office in Belgrade, the commission included about a dozen members; most were Albanian but two were Serb. The UNHCHR was well placed to chair the commission since its mandate covered all of Yugoslavia and it had offices in Belgrade and Pristina; its Belgrade representatives could report to commission members on the situation of the detainees in Serbia proper.

The commission was a useful source of information on the situation of the detainees. It also provided a chance for its members to express their grievances and to convey the urgency on the fate of the detainees. Two problems quickly became apparent. First, the commission had no power to do much about the detainees. The UNHCHR could take back information to Belgrade, have meetings with key Serbian and Yugoslav officials, and start a dialogue, but results were sparse and the families in Kosovo were getting impatient. Rallies, street demonstrations, sit-ins, and other forms of public protest became weekly features of life in Kosovo. This was especially true in Djakovica, a city from which the Serb forces had taken about 140 young men as NATO arrived. Second, the commission's Albanian members refused to take up the question of the missing minorities, especially missing Serbs, thus frustrating the Serb members.

The government in Serbia started to release some of the 1,962 Albanians recorded in their prisons by the ICRC in September 1999. However, stories about Serb and Albanian lawyers charging large fees to secure their release also surfaced. In some cases it became apparent that for the right amount of money a detainee would be released whatever the charges. This caused even more resentment in the Albanian community, but there was little the commission or UNMIK could do; in fact, some families said they would do anything to get their loved ones back and criticized their own leaders for failing to discuss the issue with Belgrade. UNMIK leaders likewise were reluctant to raise the matter directly where it mattered most, in Belgrade. By December 1999, groups of mothers of the detainees demanded to meet with SRSG Kouchner and the Human Rights Office and they did. These meetings were very emotional and difficult for all. Kouchner raised the issue constantly when he briefed the Security Council and met with the steady stream of foreign dignitaries who had added Kosovo to their itineraries. But the key to the problem resided in Belgrade and squarely with Milosevic.

Hope increased dramatically with the election of Kostunica in October 2000. Kostunica promised to get an amnesty bill through parliament that would lead to the release of most of the Albanians. Flora Brovina, a hero to Kosovo Albanians, had been convicted on trumped-up charges in a deeply flawed proceeding in December 1999. Her release in November 2000 and her immediate insistence that the remaining detainees in Serbia be released gave hope for the first time that this painful problem would be solved. Finally, on February 26, 2001, the Yugoslav parliament passed an amnesty law that would free many of the remaining Albanians in detention. The law provides amnesty to all those convicted of conspiring against the state but will not amnesty those convicted of terrorism.[16] As of January 2001, the ICRC listed 698 Kosovo Albanian detainees in Serbia proper, of whom about 450 should benefit from the amnesty. The remaining 200 were convicted of terrorism, but some on very flimsy evidence. President Kostunica has promised to review all these terrorism cases and to pardon those whose convictions appear to be unsound. By April 2001, Belgrade had released 210 Albanians based on the February amnesty law.

The question of the "missing" has always been related to the question of the detainees in Serbia, although often people have confused the two. Even the SRSG and the UN press office referred to "5,000 missing" in several public statements. The real number is about 3,600. Among them are 2,772 Albanians, 549 Serbs, 144 Roma, 57 Montenegrins, 31 Muslim Slavs, and 47 "other" (Turks, Macedonians, Gorani, not specified). The ICTY's exhumations have yielded 2,360 bodies that have been identified and 1,260 that remain unidentified. The number of missing may decrease if and when these 1,260 bodies are identified. That would leave about 2,300 people whose whereabouts are unknown and thus are "missing." Yet some Albanian leaders, for political reasons, insist that 10,000 people are missing, but this is an exaggeration. Some families understandably support the higher figure, hoping that their loved one was in some secret detention center and would be found alive; the sad but likely truth is that the person is dead. Serb leaders also encourage the belief that missing Serbs may be alive, but as noted previously by Adem Demaci, a former UCK spokesman, missing Serbs and Roma are most likely dead. Nevertheless, there is complete silence on the Kosovo Albanian side when it comes to the issue of missing Serbs, Roma, and Muslim Slavs.

The likely fate of many of the 2,300 missing persons was revealed in a most unlikely setting: a Yugoslav army court martial in April 2001. A Yugoslav paratrooper on trial for war crimes committed in Kosovo revealed the existence of a "trace-erasing unit" charged with removing evidence of mass killings during the war by body removal and burning up the remains.[17] Further evidence emerged in May 2001 when the press reported on a truck that had been filled with 89 bodies and dumped in the Danube River near the Serbian town of Kladovo in April 1999. A diver who discovered the truck and the bodies inside confirmed the account which directly implicates former President Milosevic in war crimes in Kosovo and a cover-up. Among the dead were many women, children, and elderly persons. Milosevic was shortly after handed over to the ICTY in the Hague in June 2001. Over the following weeks several mass graves of Kosovo Albanians were found in Serbia. It is highly probable that most of the remaining missing Albanians from the conflict will be found in these mass graves.[18]

UNMIK, through the OSCE, established the Victim Recovery Identification Commission (VRIC). The VRIC includes representatives from the OSCE, KFOR, CIVPOL, and the ICRC, and local representatives. The main task is to identify mortal remains uncovered in the various exhumations, including those conducted by investigators from the ICTY. The VRIC has run workshops to train Kosovars on exhumations, victim identification, and related tasks. The goal is for the VRIC to identify mortal remains so that families can know the fate of their loved ones. OSCE officials hope to hand off this work to local staff once they have received sufficient training.

Human Rights Abuses: Patterns and Responses

After the initial spasms of violence, patterns soon emerged. Responses took time to develop, largely due to an internal debate—especially within UNMIK—about the nature of the violence and who was responsible.

The OSCE had primary responsibility for monitoring human rights violations and for investigating and verifying that such violations had occurred. OSCE quickly mounted a presence throughout Kosovo and by August 1999 had field officers covering the entire territory. These officers received information about attacks, visited the scene, interviewed witnesses and victims when possible, and wrote weekly reports summarizing their findings. Officers wrote "spot reports" for serious incidents.

CIVPOL also investigated violent incidents from the moment of their deployment. Applying their professional police skills, CIVPOL proved vital in preserving the crime scene, identifying and cataloging physical evidence, and spotting trends in violent activity.

KFOR troops also played an important part in deciphering the violence. Many attacks involved weapons of war (mortars, grenades, rocket launchers, landmines) and military-type tactics. These went beyond the experience or knowledge of the average civilian human rights or police officer. In the best of circumstances, OSCE Human Rights Division, CIVPOL, and KFOR coordinated their actions, exchanged information, and assisted each other in the effort to identify the perpetrators. One OSCE human rights officer noted, "If they [KFOR and UNMIK police] didn't share their information, we wouldn't know what was going on, and we couldn't identify the human rights violation. . . . If we didn't have KFOR and UNMIK Police cooperation, it would be much more time consuming to go out there and see how it happened, why exactly it happened and look for the individual."[19]

By the end of September 1999, key leaders in OSCE Human Rights, UNHCR, CIVPOL, and KFOR joined me in concluding that much more was involved than mere revenge attacks, violence engendered by some wrong suffered in the past, or common crime. There was clearly an organized campaign—premeditated, structured, equipped, and directed to attacking Serbs and Roma and other minorities simply because of their ethnicity. No proof or even indication of prior participation in the persecution of Albanians was necessary; simply belonging to the targeted ethnic group was enough. Turks and Muslim Slavs were also at risk, though the degree of threat varied.

The OSCE decided to document comprehensively the extent of the violence plaguing Kosovo by compiling all the information it had gathered since its return in early June. All field offices started to comb their files and categorize the attacks, including only those that had been verified; some cases required further investigations, which were duly undertaken. Some allegations could not be verified and these cases were thrown out.

The result was a 300-page report that makes for harrowing reading.[20] The report documents cases of murder, disappearances/abductions, torture, beatings, arbitrary arrests and detention, and severe restrictions on freedom of movement and expression. House burnings and looting in every part of Kosovo are recorded; this includes Serb extremists in northern Mitrovica targeting the Albanian and Bosniak minorities there. Also disturbing were violations of economic, social, and cultural rights uncovered by the OSCE monitors. Cases of routine and systematic discrimination in providing heath care, unequal treatment in the distribution of humanitarian assistance, and limited access to basic public services were rife.

The care and level of detail, the corroboration, and the moderate tone of the report make it a powerful indictment of the Kosovo Albanian leadership's failure to control extremists in its ranks. The cumulative impact of such overwhelming evidence points to a concerted campaign to expel from Kosovo most of its ethnic minorities, especially Serbs. No Kosovo Albanian of any stature had convincingly condemned this campaign for many months. One leading Kosovo Albanian analyst said that the criticisms of violence by the leadership "rarely went beyond the walls of the room where the meetings took place in UNMIK headquarters." Such condemnations were usually made in English and posted on websites but were not translated into Albanian or disseminated in the local media. Moreover, the Albanian hard-liners took advantage of confusion in the ranks of UNMIK on the question of the nature of the violence against minorities to continue their campaign. They saw no convincing evidence that they would be held accountable as purported leaders of society.

UNMIK senior leadership, including the SRSG, expressed disgust in private at the ongoing violence documented in the OSCE's report. Public condemnations were also forthcoming, but usually with several qualifiers. UNMIK leadership would not mention the current violations without referring to the past, especially the recent attempt at ethnic cleansing by the Serbian authorities and the "ten years of apartheid" before that. UNMIK press releases and official statements usually included references to Northern Ireland and South Africa and the difficult nature of reconciliation following a conflict. This constant reminder to "understand the context" and "to realize what they have been through" was interpreted by the Albanian hard-liners as at least a yellow light to continue their violent campaign.

Some in UNMIK even questioned whether the violence was indeed planned; they asserted that these incidents were random, spontaneous outbursts of an aggrieved people against their former oppressors. The SRSG's foreword to the OSCE report reflected the debate within UNMIK on this question. The initial draft by the SRSG's Human Rights Office stated that "armed groups seem to operate in an organized fashion and have some form of hierarchy, command and control."[21] A paragraph drafted by others in the SRSG's office several pages later contradicts this assertion, saying, "The crimes we see are acts of individuals."[22]

Excuses were made for the UCK and its leaders, especially Hasim Thaci and Agim Ceku, when case after case documented by the OSCE, CIVPOL, and KFOR showed that UCK or former UCK members were implicated in most of the serious incidents. The response was: Even if it is the UCK, and we don't know if it is, it could just be people wearing UCK uniforms; it's not Thaci's or Ceku's fault because they can't control these guys. The alleged lack of control over rogue elements is a frequent alibi for insurgents, commonly known as "plausible deniability," and begs a larger question. If Thaci, Haradinaj, Ceku, and others could not control their people, then why was anyone wasting any time talking to them? The same holds true for leaders of the Serbian community. They either represented something or they didn't. Power means accountability. They could not have it both ways—that is, be leaders of a guerrilla army or political movement and yet not be responsible for its actions. While regional loyalties and clan identification made the UCK less of a well-oiled and totally disciplined machine than the German Wehrmacht, neither was it the loose amalgam of uncontrollable bands that its now former leaders or apologists would like people to believe. If every shop could close on Albanian Flag Day on November 29, 1999, all over Kosovo, then the violence could be shut off or turned on with the same efficiency.

While violence has fluctuated since UNMIK/KFOR rule began in June 1999, the corrosive effect of violence, fear, and intimidation has not. Despite many innovative efforts and the commitment of thousands of international civilians and military, security for minorities and moderates remains elusive. UNHCR, in a gloomy but accurate assessment made in August 2001, noted:

> UNHCR remains, however, extremely concerned that even now, more than 2 years after the entry of the international community into Kosovo, there is no freedom of movement for the majority of the minority communities, there is no guarantee of security for any non-Albanian (not even for all k/Albanians) and attacks on complete innocent members of the minority population continue. Just looking through the police reports of the past month, arson, shooting incidents, and assaults directed at members of the Serbian, RAE [Roma, Ashkalia, and Egyptian], Bosniak and Gorani communities continue to happen on a daily basis. Even refugees from FYROM have been targeted. Return of all communities to Kosovo is being hampered by these incidents, and so is the creation of a multi-ethnic society that strives to achieve an autonomous status.[23]

A summary of the more egregious cases found in the OSCE report released in December 1999, and later cases, shows both the planned, organized nature of the violence and the involvement of UCK personnel (military and PU/UCK police). In the case of Serb-controlled northern Kosovo, the OSCE analyzes the role and responsibility of highly organized groups of Serb police and paramilitaries.

The Violence in Kosovo: Regional Analysis

Gnjilane. The OCSE report documents cases of executions, disappearances, arbitrary arrest and detention, house burnings and evictions, shooting/grenade/mortar attacks, and widespread discrimination in economic life, access to education, and medical care in the Gnjilane area. This violence was most intense in the weeks immediately following KFOR's entry but persisted throughout. Violence came in clusters, which OSCE analysts interpreted as being "suggestive of a degree of planning, or of cells operating at certain times in certain areas, and the September cases in particular are suggestive of the organized targeting of a specific group."[24] An example of this type of planning occurred between October 17 and 22, 1999, when a series of grenade attacks against Serb houses and stores occurred in Gnjilane town. These attacks were followed by arson of Serb houses. KFOR then arrested several former UCK members.[25]

OSCE also received numerous reports of UCK members, or people dressed in UCK uniforms and identifying themselves as such, involved in a pattern of arrests and detention, often accompanied by beatings of the detainees. Eight people interviewed by the OSCE claimed they had been interrogated at UCK headquarters in Gnjilane. Every report of ill treatment from June 19 to July 1, 1999, alleged that the UCK were the perpetrators.

The harassment and violence extended beyond Serbs, Roma, and other minorities. Albanians, especially members of Rugova's LDK Party, were told to cease their political activities; but the fear was so great that OSCE and KFOR found it very difficult to get anyone to file a complaint or to identify those responsible. Albanian shopkeepers who served Serbs were warned to stop or they would be fined, or worse. OSCE officers found a circular sent to all shops from the illegal self-styled Municipality Council of Gnjilane, Directorate of Economy and Finance, Tax Branch, ordering a payment of a 10 percent tax on all stock and inventory. This was extortion, pure and simple.

The violence has continued throughout 2000 and into 2001. Serb houses in Vitina have been destroyed, an ancient Serbian Orthodox church has been burned to the ground, and several violent attacks against Serbs have resulted in deaths and serious injuries. The area became even more tense in the fall of 2000 with an upsurge in activity by the Army for the Liberation of Presevo, Medvedja, and Bujanovac (UCPMB), an offshoot of the UCK fighting to attach those southern Serbia areas to Kosovo.

Pec. The town and region suffered heavy damage during the war from both the Serb forces and NATO bombing. Most minorities had fled by the time KFOR arrived, but those who remained reported constant threats, harassment, or worse. Most alleged that UCK were responsible, although here as elsewhere some perpetrators may have been using UCK uniforms or badges as a cover. OSCE noted, however, that "some UCK control was being exerted. . . . In many cases the victims reported that once they had asked the (now former) UCK to intervene, the threats or harassment stopped."[26]

The OSCE officers in Pec obtained a revealing set of responses from a UCK zone commander in Dukagjini when they asked him about the violence perpetrated against the dwindling number of minorities in his region. He said:

1. How can you expect me to do anything as long as my people do not have roofs over their heads?

2. We no longer have policing powers; KFOR will have to deal with this.
3. I will not make any public statement against any revenge action unless directed to do so by Agim Ceku [former head of the UCK military and now commanding officer of the TMK].
4. It is not UCK. Anyway, we do not have a policy of killing people. We have a policy of killing the Serb interest in Kosovo.
5. There is a difference between Serbs and other minorities. I will not deal with Serbs, but other groups sometimes approached us for help and sometimes we help.
6. Anyway, my priority is my people. I have to take care of 1,400 soldiers and their families and the families of 400 who died. When that is taken care of we can look to other areas.[27]

Every case of killing, disappearance, or beating for the Djakovica region in the OSCE report involves UCK, people identifying themselves as UCK or wearing UCK uniforms. In Istok municipality, known UCK members took part in rounding up Serbs, who were never seen alive again; UCK also intimidated Roma in the area. In September 1999, a Kosovo Albanian was interrogated by UCK members on suspicion that he had passed information to the Serbs during the war and that he had Serb friends, apparently a criminal offense.

Self-styled municipal authorities took over many government functions in the Pec region while the cumbersome UN bureaucracy failed to field administrators for months. In this vacuum the authorities issued license plates, tried to collect taxes, and evicted people from apartments. Forced evictions of Roma continued for months, but even Albanians were evicted to make room for UCK "war heroes." "The UCK is a plague, they are involved in every illegal activity," said a UN official familiar with the city.[28] Although formally disbanded in September 1999, the UCK structure and authority remained intact.

The OSCE analysis of the human rights situation in the west of Kosovo

revealed a striking number of cases with alleged UCK or provisional TMK involvement. A general atmosphere of intimidation prevented some people from giving full accounts and there is a high probability that many incidents were never reported, but in total, the (now former) UCK were alleged to have been involved in 33 cases. From killing to eviction and tax collection, there were apparently few areas into which the power and control of the UCK/provisional TMK allied to the self-styled administration, did not reach.[29]

While the commander of the UCK claimed that it was imposters or opportunists using the UCK as cover, he or the real UCK did not attempt to identify or even help KFOR troops apprehend the perpetrators. Yet it would have been in the UCK's interest to remove this stigma and suspicion. This failure casts serious doubt on the commander's claim, which sounds more like a convenient excuse exploiting the "plausible deniability" so common in these circumstances.

Pristina. The Gnjilane region has seen some of the worst human rights violations since the arrival of UNMIK and KFOR. It started early in their tenure: on July 23 in the village of Gracko, a KFOR patrol heard gunfire around 11 P.M. Arriving on the scene, they found fourteen dead bodies, all Serb males between the ages of fifteen and sixty. They had gone to harvest their fields nearby; their families said they had asked for KFOR protection but KFOR declined, saying they did not have enough personnel. All the bodies except one were found close together. Several Kosovo Albanians were arrested, and a search of their houses yielded various weapons. All but one were later released. This incident terrified the remaining Serbs in the area.

Lipljan municipality saw a well-planned, systematic grenade attack on Serbs and their houses. Lipljan has several villages with mixed populations, and the town itself has Serbs and Roma. OSCE found that between July 9 and August 7, 1999, there were thirty grenade attacks and related incidents in the town. Sixteen people were arrested, all Albanians. Their tactic was to have a male and female walk together, with the female carrying the grenade; KFOR troops at this point rarely searched females. When the couple arrived at the target, the female would hand the grenade to the male, who would throw it, and then they would escape. This carefully planned, premeditated violence is the antithesis of "spasms of uncontrollable revenge." Once the arrests were made, grenade attacks practically stopped. Yet all the suspects were released by the Albanian-dominated judiciary for lack of evidence. After their release, there were nine grenade attacks. A sustained and organized grenade attack on Roma homes occurred in October 1999, when four houses were damaged in villages outside Lipljan.

In addition to the killings, grenade attacks, and severe restriction of movement for minorities, abductions have intensified the fears of those remaining. In Urosevac/Ferizaj, several Roma men were abducted in October 1999; their families suspect UCK were responsible. In Pristina itself, a spate of abductions of Serbs occurred in August and September 1999, leading to increased security measures adopted by British KFOR, who deployed twenty-four-hour guards to Serb apartments or houses scattered around the city. Two Serb teachers from Strpce were abducted when they went to Urosevac on September 28 to meet their Albanian colleagues. They have never been seen again. Their disappearance led to violent demonstrations against KFOR and UNMIK in Strpce. OSCE noted that these disappearances have a cumulative and pernicious impact on an already fearful community, reinforcing a bunker mentality and restricting even further their freedom of movement. Serbs and most Roma now fear leaving their enclaves without KFOR escort. To do otherwise is to risk death.

Pristina, as the seat of many government institutions and large business enterprises, was a ripe target for reverse ethnic discrimination. While the Serbs dominated these sectors in the era of stripped autonomy, Albanian hard-liners made sure that the Serbs would now suffer. The Pristina hospital became a dangerous place for Serbs and Roma to seek care. One Albanian doctor, quoted as saying, "They treated us like dogs, now we will treat them like dogs," refused to give a painkiller to a Serb who needed stitches.[30] Serbs and Roma soon stopped seeking treatment at the hospital; people with serious cases had to go as far as Nis in southern Serbia for treatment.

Employment discrimination was rife. Serb employees in television, radio, power, and water supply were told not to come to work, or they soon became too afraid to do so. The discrimination extended to Albanians not deemed to be sufficiently pro-UCK. The UCK opposed the hiring of any LDK members in Stimle municipality.

Apartment evictions soon became a serious problem in Pristina as people flooded into the city seeking jobs and shelter.[31] Many from the countryside had lost their homes to the bombing or Serb destruction. The entire Roma quarter in Obilic was torched and Serb houses were routinely burned.

UCK police issued illegal eviction orders to coerce minorities to leave or else. Albanians who had agreed to look after the apartments of Serb friends who had been forced to leave were threatened by the UCK police, who demanded that the Albanians turn over their apartments. In one case, the Albanian family was given twelve hours to leave. A KFOR patrol came across two UCK police in the midst of trying to evict an Albanian family. The men admitted they were UCK and even produced an identity card that said on the reverse side:

> The bearer of this official ID is an officially authorized person that has weapons, and can use them as mentioned by law; to detain persons, and bring them to police stations; to get access into apartments without warning; to use other persons' vehicles for transport and phones; to confiscate goods that are contraband.[32]

This UCK police force was illegal; only KFOR and UNMIK police had the legal authority to make arrests. Yet this incident reveals just how organized and pervasive the UCK were during the first year of KFOR and UNMIK's presence in Kosovo. It has proven very difficult to root out this parallel police force.

Mitrovica. The divided city of Mitrovica is the most photographed locale in Kosovo. Heavily armed KFOR soldiers guard the bridge over the Ibar

River separating the Serb north from the Albanian south. Crossing into northern Mitrovica is like leaving one country and entering another. The signs are in Cyrillic, and Serb turbo-rock music or folk songs blare from loudspeakers. Yugoslav dinars, not seen now in the rest of Kosovo, are the currency of choice. Cars with license plates from Belgrade and other parts of Serbia line the streets. The north is much poorer than the south and goods are scarce; you even see breadlines outside the few functioning bakeries.

Northern Mitrovica also shows that Serb extremists try to control their population just as Albanian hard-liners do in the south. In the south, the UCK police and provisional TMK performed police functions in the early months following the end of the NATO air campaign; in the north, Serb police and paramilitary were present. It took many months for KFOR and then the UN police to deploy in sufficient numbers to sideline these illegal policing activities on both sides.

OSCE reported from the summer of 1999 the presence of "bridge watchers" in the north. This group, largely physically fit, military-type young men, sat in a café at the northern end of the bridge and watched everyone who was allowed to cross the KFOR checkpoint into the north. Sentries were also posted on tall apartment buildings, and using walkie-talkies, the bridge watchers could mobilize a crowd of several hundred people in a matter of minutes. The first time I walked across the bridge in early September 1999, two young Albanian males also tried to walk across. A howl went up from the bridge watchers, who menacingly approached the young men; French KFOR quickly whisked the two away to a building for questioning, and they were soon turned back. This incident clearly showed the Serb extremists' organization and readiness to use violence to preserve the separation of the city.

In the south, the UCK-dominated self-appointed administration controlled most aspects of daily life. OSCE officers noted that "its degree of control was demonstrated on several occasions when a call from the self-styled administration to cease demonstrations or violence resulted in almost immediate calm," citing a rally to support Albanian returns to Brdo/Vitakut, where calm was restored within an hour after the Albanian leadership's request.[33]

Leadership on both sides have called and ended demonstrations at will. Albanian men often formed at the southern side of the bridge and would attempt to cross the bridge, only to be prevented by KFOR. Frustration and tension mounted as the separation solidified. On August 4, 1999, rockets and grenades were fired from the south to the north damaging several apartments facing the river. In September, the total breakdown over sharing the only hospital, which is in the north, only heightened the enmity. The dispute over mixed schools followed, with Albanians insisting that they had to have access to the university and technical school in the north and the Serbs resisting this idea. Demonstrations, again called quickly and ending just as fast, ensued. The only result was segregated, not mixed, schools and increased bitterness all around. Mitrovica was a microcosm of Kosovo, but other municipalities in the north fared no better. Security concerns predominate and limit freedom of movement for all in northern Kosovo; discrimination in access to all public services is also the norm.

The Albanian and Serb extremists are each other's most important allies; one side's actions reinforces and "justifies" the other's violence. They literally feed off each other, and KFOR and various UNMIK administrators have not figured out how to break this unholy dynamic.

In southern Mitrovica and the municipalities of Vucitrn and Srbica, the now depressingly familiar pattern of tight control by UCK and provisional TMK was repeated. The large Roma quarter in southern Mitrovica, which formerly housed 5,000 Roma, was burned to the ground. Children were sometimes used to set these fires because the parents knew that KFOR was unlikely either to suspect or to arrest kids. This tactic would be used elsewhere in Kosovo with devastating effect on the healthy development of children, reinforcing hatred and making reconciliation even more difficult. Harassment of Muslim Slavs increased: one male disappeared without a trace and several women were beaten. UCK police were accused in many of these cases. The provisional TMK took over a main official building in downtown Vucitrn and made no attempt to hide its presence, unfurling a large Albanian flag at the entry. Similarly, in Srbica in the Drenica Valley, the birthplace of the UCK, the provisional TMK adopted a robust and public presence. They conducted policing activities, including arrest, detention, and interrogation; LDK members were harassed here as elsewhere.

Throughout July–October 1999, numerous attacks against Serbs in their few enclaves in the south caused death and great fear. Roma too were targeted, especially in Vucitrn, where one family endured at least three grenade attacks. The train linking several Serb villages to Zvecan in the north and Kosovo Polje in the south was stoned regularly and derailed on July 20 and September 26, 2000.

Prizren. The town of Prizren and the surrounding region had one of the most ethnically diverse populations in Kosovo before the war. This is no longer the case, as almost all Serbs and most Roma have fled. Muslim Slavs and Turks face severe intimidation and threats.

UCK and provisional TMK conducted policing activities in the region, even after UNMIK police assumed police primacy on October 27, 1999. "Men in black" or in camouflage took people to known UCK buildings for "informative talks," which usually included beatings and severe mistreatment. UCK appointees took over key administrative posts in the self-styled administrations in the southern municipalities early on and proved extremely difficult to dislodge. In one case, even after the UN administrator had arrived in Suva Reka, the UCK appointee refused to yield and beat the official following an argument. The man was arrested but then quickly released by the local judiciary. Birth and death certificates, marriage licenses, car registration, and, of course, illegal taxes were all part of this parallel administration in Prizren, Suva Reka, Gora, and Orahovac municipalities.

The blockade around Orahovac to protest deployment of Russian troops and the presence of suspected war criminals among the Serb population in Orahovac made this town especially tense in the first nine months following NATO's entry. As of October 1999, six Roma and fifteen Serbs had "disappeared" from the municipality. In most cases, eyewitnesses claim that UCK or men in UCK uniforms were responsible.

KFOR has arrested eleven Serbs on war crimes charges from Orahovac. Five were arrested as they tried to leave Kosovo in a convoy organized by UNHCR to seek medical attention unobtainable for Serbs in Kosovo due to security risks. After being cleared by UNHCR, the list of those to be on the bus was given to KFOR. Without UNHCR's knowledge, KFOR checked this list against its own list of war crimes suspects. Five matches were found, and once the convoy was about to leave, the five were taken off the bus and detained by KFOR. This caused an uproar in the Serb community and put UNHCR staff at risk. Serbs accused UNHCR of secretly collaborating with KFOR to arrest Serbs, and its ability to work in Orahovac was threatened. UNHCR protested vehemently to KFOR saying that this was unacceptable and that UNHCR could not be seen as a decoy or an agent of KFOR to arrest suspected war criminals. KFOR later agreed that it would not make arrests from convoys.

In Dragash, the administrative seat of Gora municipality, a concerted effort to force the Muslim Slavs to leave began in October 1999. Grenades thrown into the yards and houses of Muslim Slavs was the not-so-subtle hint. Fear prevented many Muslim Slavs from providing information about the attacks after many received anonymous threatening phone calls. In one case, while an OSCE team attempted to interview one victim, a team of provisional TMK members appeared and observed the discussion.[34]

Education became a key human rights issue. Some self-appointed officials refused to allow any instruction in Serbian, even though UNMIK declared Serbian one of the official languages of instruction. Threats were made against teachers or parents who insisted on this right. Many Muslim Slav families either left or did not register their children for school, because the only option offered to them was schooling in Albanian, which their children did not speak.

House burnings and evictions were common in the Prizren region. KFOR military police reported thirty-six incidents of forced evictions in

August and September 1999 involving UCK or provisional TMK. More damage to housing was inflicted in Prizren after the war than during it. More than 300 houses, predominantly Serb-owned, have burned; the obvious motive is to prevent Serbs from returning. In one case, three men in UCK uniform attacked a fireman trying to put out a blaze.

A disturbing feature of the postwar violence in the Prizren area and elsewhere in Kosovo is the targeted attacks on the elderly. The OSCE recorded the murders of nineteen Serbs in the Prizren region who were over sixty-five years old; seventeen elderly Serbs went missing from the village of Dojnice and their bodies have never been found. Undoubtedly there are other unrecorded cases. In a number of instances, young children, twelve to fifteen years old, have harassed and attacked the elderly.

UNMIK's Joint Task Force on Minorities had identified a serious problem in the Zupa Valley northeast of Prizren town in the fall of 1999. Men and women, predominantly Serb but also including Muslim Slavs, who were over sixty-five years old were targeted in several villages in the valley. The patrols that KFOR sent to these villages were greatly appreciated but not sufficient. The task force includes the joint chairs—OSCE and UNHCR—and representatives from KFOR, CIVPOL, OHCHR, ICRC, UNICEF, UNMIK's Pillar Two (Civil Administration), and the senior adviser on human rights to the SRSG. The task force has issued regular reports on the situation for minorities in Kosovo, each a wealth of detail and revealing an ongoing climate of fear and danger and a growing self-segregation for the sake of survival among Kosovo's remaining minorities. It is the most effective example of interagency cooperation that I have ever seen in a peacekeeping operation. The task force decided to send me to the area to collect facts about the attacks and report back to it with a plan of action.

I visited several of the villages on October 21, 1999, accompanied by staff from OSCE/Human Rights' Prizren office. We met with several elderly Serb women who were completely terrified, and with good reason. Two of them had recently been severely beaten. One woman's face was still swollen badly and she had black and blue marks on her neck—ten days after the beating. A ninety-six-year-old man was beaten to death in one of the villages on September 15; his body was found in his house with his hands tied behind his back and a strap tied across his mouth. Everyone we met with begged for more KFOR protection. They feared for their lives. In some cases, the alleged perpetrators were arrested, later released, and seen again in the area soon after.

The soldiers of a German KFOR patrol we met said they wanted to do more to protect the villagers. So far, they could only patrol, and everyone knew that the perpetrators of these crimes and human rights violations only waited for the patrols to leave and then returned to terrorize, beat, kill, and steal. In one village, we came upon three men who were stealing bees, hives, and honey from the hives; this is not trivial, as honey production is one of the few income-producing activities left in the area. We were able to stop them, get the license plate number of their truck, and alert KFOR who came and questioned the men.

Following this visit I wrote a memo to the SRSG explaining the situation and recommending that KFOR place a checkpoint on the one road leading to and from the villages. The deputy SRSG for humanitarian assistance (Dennis McNamara) also visited the villages within days and delivered a similar recommendation to the SRSG. The principal deputy SRSG then met with the KFOR commander, who agreed to allow Turkish KFOR to erect a checkpoint. German KFOR increased their mobile patrols and varied the timing to make them unpredictable. The attacks stopped. This was an example of task force action yielding real results.

A second issue that emerged from the Zupa Valley investigation was the increase in threats made by former UCK against Slavic Muslims concerning the distribution of humanitarian assistance. OSCE and UNHCR field officers received consistent and reliable reports that former UCK warned Slavic Muslims not to share with their Serb neighbors the humanitarian assistance they received from international agencies. If they did, the Slavic Muslims' houses would be burned or worse. Slavic Muslim shopowners have also been told not to sell to Serbs or else they will suffer the consequences.

Again, the checkpoint prevented those who were making the threats from carrying them out, and KFOR deployed more robustly to ensure that humanitarian assistance was distributed without discrimination. This helped alleviate a terrible dilemma many Slavic Muslims faced: many wanted to help their Serb neighbors but had risked their lives in doing so.

The OSCE report quotes a local saying, "As Prizren goes, so goes Kosovo." This is not good news for either Prizren or Kosovo. Control by extremists seeking to impose "ethnic purity" is not what most Kosovars want or why the international community intervened. The OSCE concluded that "what is clear is that the atmosphere in Prizren provided the space and freedom for a consistent campaign of harassment aimed at driving out the remaining minorities and the purported leaders of the community did nothing to even stop or condemn this campaign."[35]

UCK personnel, provisional TMK, and self-styled authorities made no effort to stop the violence or even to condemn it convincingly. The only inference to be drawn from repeated attacks in the same areas in the same way at the same time with the same targeted population is that Albanian leaders who could have stopped the violence had no interest in doing so. This was an organized, systematic effort to rid Prizren of its minority population.

If the UCK and provisional TMK would not stop the violence, could

KFOR and the UN have done more? And what can they do now to improve security and create some semblance of the rule of law?

NOTES

1. This was also true in Europe following World War II, where those accused of having collaborated with the Nazi regime often faced various forms of summary justice, including executions by mobs, beatings, and public humiliation.

2. Steven Erlanger, "Aide Takes Stock of UN in Kosovo," *New York Times,* July 17, 2000.

3. Christophe Chatelot, "Hate and Fear Stalk Kosovo's Dwindling Serbs," *Le Monde,* reprinted in the *Guardian Weekly,* July 13–19, 2000, p. 28.

4. Quoted in Michael Kelly, "Anarchy in Kosovo," *Washington Post,* March 22, 2000.

5. Sebastian Junger, "A Different Kind of Killing," *New York Times Magazine,* February 27, 2000, p. 88.

6. *Guardian* journalist Jonathan Steele makes a similar mistake describing the violence by Albanians as the "revenge-seeking of a bereaved people returning to destroyed villages and burning the houses of their Serbian neighbors," and not as an organized campaign of ethnic cleansing by a ruthless core of Albanian extremists. See "Search for a Safe Harbour," *Guardian Weekly,* March 30–April 3, 2000.

7. Institute for War and Peace Reporting, "Tribunal Update 200: Last Week in the Hague (November 20–25, 2000)," available at http://www.iwpr.net/index.pl5?archive/tri/tri_200_4_eng.txt.

8. "Head of UN Mission in Kosovo Vows to Find Killers of Ashkali Returnees," UN News, UNMIK website, November 10, 2000, www.un.org/peace/kosovo/pages; Steven Erlanger, "A Freed Albanian Visits Restive Serb Prisons," *New York Times,* November 10, 2000, p. A14. Ironically, the four killed were "Ashkalia," Albanian-speaking Roma who regard themselves as closer to Albanians than to Serbs. This did not protect them in this case. A few days later, a thirteen-year-old Ashkalia boy was burned to death when he returned to Orahovac to inspect his family's abandoned house.

9. See Michael Ignatieff, *Virtual War: Kosovo and Beyond* (New York: Henry Holt, 2000).

10. Quoted in William J. Byron, S.J., *Jesuit Saturdays: Sharing the Ignatian Spirit with Lay Colleagues and Friends* (Chicago: Loyola Press, 2000), p. 58.

11. Some Serbs argue that they should not have to apologize if they did not commit any crimes themselves. Yet an apology "often serves as a catalyst for change, for movement towards reconciliation. It is not an admission of guilt, but a taking of responsibility for one's past. . . . But the apology must come first, establishing the political conditions for anything that might follow." Simon Chesterman, "Seating Arrangements at the Table of World Morality" (reviewing Elazar Barkan, *The Guilt of Nations: Restitution and Negotiating Historical Injustices*) *London Review of Books,* October 19, 2000, p. 30.

12. Zubin Potok, Zvecan, and Leposavic.

13. I use the term "Roma" to refer to all three unless the specific case requires otherwise.

14. UNMIK Press Briefing, March 7, 2001, available at www.org/peace/kosovo/briefing/pressbrief7March01.

15. AP "Fate of Kosovo Albanian Prisoners Key to Peace in Yugoslavia," *Associated Press,* November 3, 2000.

16. Carlotta Gall, "Yugoslav Parliament Passes Amnesty for Jailed Kosovars," *New York Times,* February 27, 2001.

17. John Sweeney, "Yugoslav Court Martial Reveals Serb War Crime," *Guardian Weekly,* April 26–May 2, 2001.

18. Carlotta Gall, "A Dark Secret Comes to Light in Serbia," *New York Times,* June 1, 2001.

19. Katarina Mansson, "Co-operation in Human Rights: Experience from the Peacekeeping Operation in Kosovo" (master's thesis, 2000), p. 43, quoting from an interview with an OSCE human rights field officer.

20. OSCE, *Kosovo/Kosova: As Seen, As Told,* part 2, Report on *Human Rights Findings of the OSCE Mission in Kosovo, June to October 1999,* (Warsaw: OSCE, 1999)

21. Ibid., p. iii.

22. Ibid., p. vi.

23. UNMIK press briefing, Aug. 9, 2001, available online at http://www.un.org/peace/kosovo/briefing/pressbrief9aug01.htm.

24. OSCE Report, *As Seen, As Told,* part 2.

25. Ibid., p. 38.

26. Ibid., p. 50.

27. Ibid.

28. Interview, New York, November 20, 2000.

29. OSCE, *As Seen, As Told,* part 2, p. 61. The provisional TMK is the successor corps to the UCK. It was "provisional" until January 21, 2000, when the first members of the TMK were sworn in. Until then, applicants received cards identifying them as TMK candidates. This is discussed further in Chapter 8.

30. Ibid., p. 72. This same doctor reportedly refused to treat a Serb woman with gunshot wounds, telling her that she should go to her local medical center and that Pristina hospital would not provide transportation.

31. Even though KFOR and OSCE human rights officers in 1999 identified apartment evictions and property disputes as a key human rights issue that could and did lead to serious violence, UNMIK did not get a property claims commission operating until mid-2001. In July 2001, UNMIK issued a regulation requiring an official review of all property sales between ethnic groups to ensure that the transfer is voluntary. This review process is meant to prevent slow-motion ethnic cleansing by intimidation. OSCE and UNHCR had reported for months that Albanian extremists were pressuring Serbs to sell their properties, threatening violence and outright expropriation if the owner refused.

32. OSCE, *As Seen, As Told,* part 2, p. 84.

33. Ibid., p. 91.

34. Ibid., p. 119.

35. Ibid., p. 126.

6

The Kosovo Judiciary
and Legal Reform

STEPPING INTO THE VOID

KFOR troops encountered a lawless state when they entered Kosovo in June 1999, and, as we have seen, revenge attacks began immediately. The local judiciary dissolved. Most were Serbs who, fearing retribution, fled to Serbia proper. Some Albanians had worked in the Serb-dominated judiciary during 1989–1999, but they too feared revenge since the rest of the Albanians saw them as traitors. Virtually no judges, prosecutors, defense lawyers, or jailers were left once NATO troops arrived. Those fleeing also took whatever they could carry and destroyed what remained. The Serbs took official vehicles, computers, printers, phones, copiers, law books, court files, even office furniture with them. Court buildings looked as if a plague of heavily armed locusts had swept through, scouring the grounds for anything valuable and leaving broken windows and ripped-out electrical sockets in their wake.

Given this mayhem and void, UNMIK and KFOR should have declared martial law. If ever the conditions justified emergency rule, Kosovo from June to December 1999 was it. Serious and widespread violence, an ongoing conflict in the southern and northern sections with weapons of war used almost daily, no functioning police force—local or international—for months in various parts of the province, and a defunct court system created conditions ideal for violence. Impunity was almost guaranteed in these circumstances, so those bent on violence could carry out their campaign with little fear of being arrested and even less chance of being convicted and serving jail time. The desire for revenge fed on the lawlessness and impunity.

Martial law, with carefully circumscribed limitations on certain human rights, as permitted under international law, would have lowered the violence and sent a clear message to the UCK and Serb hard-liners that their

75

behavior would not be tolerated and that they would be punished.[1] Establishing this policy clearly and early, in the view of many Albanians interviewed, would have increased the chance for moderates to prevail, for minorities to stay, and for most Kosovars to enjoy their rights. "They were too ready to compromise, KFOR should have clamped down much harder on crime, now organized crime has really taken root."[2] Another Albanian said that UNMIK and KFOR should have declared at the outset to the Albanian population, "We are here for you. But there will be no more violence; we expect you to be mature, no revenge, that is final." An Albanian analyst added, "A vacuum existed after the 12th of June that created the fundamental conditions for lawlessness in Kosovo. A political class surfaced, led by the KLA, to fill this vacuum."

KFOR to its credit did try to create some order. Its troops in some sectors arrested people for looting and arson. This was especially true in the British sector in central Kosovo. One important lesson emerged early, although it was not applied quickly or uniformly. Strict enforcement of clear rules brings results. Where KFOR was tough but fair, the violence tended to diminish.[3]

The problems began once KFOR had detained a suspect. Now, what to do with him (it was almost always a male perpetrator, few women were arrested at this time)? There was no functioning Kosovo judiciary. KFOR tried its best to adhere to international human rights law, which prohibits long pretrial detention. But KFOR did not want to get into the business of holding detainees for extended periods and had even more concerns about being responsible for administering justice. Yet there was no one else to take up these cases, and the arrests started to pile up as the violence mushroomed.

One of the clearest lessons from earlier peacekeeping operations repeated endlessly at numerous conferences is that getting the legal system working should be a top priority in any postconflict situation. If the courts are not functioning, the entire security situation is jeopardized. Criminals roam free, the rule of law does not take hold, the most ruthless become the most influential, humanitarian assistance is diverted, and every reconstruction effort is at risk. This is precisely what happened in Kosovo. The longer the situation prevails, the harder it is to reverse course. The International Force in East Timor (INTERFET) learned this lesson from Kosovo. INTERFET established a legal regime, largely based on Indonesian law, but fully consistent with the Geneva Conventions, during the transition from Indonesian to UN rule. INTERFET and UN Civilian Police followed clear and consistent procedures governing arrest, detention, access to counsel, prison conditions, and related issues, thus avoiding the confusion faced earlier by their counterparts in Kosovo.[4] Previously, the UN Transitional Administration in Cambodia in the early 1990s created and applied a model penal code and code of criminal procedure during its mission.

EMERGENCY JUSTICE PROGRAM

UNMIK was not prepared to deal with the judicial crisis. The UN had not planned for a judicial vacuum; personnel, equipment, and a strategy were lacking. An ad hoc and reactive approach responding to the latest emergency became the operating mode. On June 28, 1999, the acting SRSG issued an emergency decree creating the Joint Advisory Council on Provisional Judicial Appointments (JAC/PJA) to identify and recommend candidates to be appointed as judges and prosecutors.[5] Working very quickly, with little chance to vet candidates thoroughly, the JAC recommended initially fifty-five judges and prosecutors during July–October.

Three problems became clear. Kosovo Serbs found it difficult and dangerous to serve. Their freedom of movement was so circumscribed that they could hardly move without armed KFOR escort. Some Serbs also felt intimidated by Serbian extremists who accused them of collaborating with the UN and the now Albanian-dominated judiciary. The Belgrade government made its unhappiness known. All seven remaining Serb judges and prosecutors soon resigned or fled from Kosovo. A virtually monoethnic judiciary composed largely of Albanians emerged. This damaged the legal system's credibility and convinced minorities that they could not get a fair hearing.

Second, the Albanians chosen had not worked in the judiciary for at least ten years. Whether through boycott or expulsion, they had lost ten years of professional growth and experience, and some were simply poorly qualified to work in such a charged and stressful atmosphere.[6] One experienced Kosovo Albanian lawyer with extensive international experience noted, "Some good judges have been appointed, but they are people coming out of a totalitarian system, which is like a diver coming from the deep sea to the surface too quickly, he gulps oxygen but his brain doesn't function normally."[7]

Third, the complete absence of the basic materials and equipment necessary to the working of courts made it difficult for everyone, regardless of ethnicity. Cars, typewriters, case files, pens, paper, phones, copiers—everything was missing and everything was needed. Yet the UN had not anticipated this need and there was little in the budget to get the system started.

Once again, KFOR came through. In early July, the first mobile courts began operations. These units, composed of judges, prosecutors, secretaries, and in some cases defense lawyers and interpreters, went to all parts of Kosovo because there was not a working courthouse in the territory for weeks. KFOR transported these mobile courts and provided security. They concentrated on holding hearings for those in KFOR detention. Under Yugoslav and international human rights law, pretrial detention must be limited in time; according to one interpretation of Yugoslav law, a judicial hearing must be held within seventy-two hours of arrest. KFOR endeavored to hold hearings in this time period, and hearings took place in the U.S. military detention center in Camp Bondsteel and in the British site near Lipljan three or four times a week. Despite this accelerated rhythm, numerous detainees were held beyond the seventy-two-hour limit.

Another problem related to detention surfaced in mid-December 1999. When KFOR started detaining people when it entered Kosovo in June, according to applicable Yugoslav federal law, the judiciary had six months maximum to conduct an investigation and then either issue an indictment or release the detainee.[8] By December, the six-month period was expiring for numerous suspects, and they would have to be indicted or released. Several suspects were deemed highly dangerous by UNMIK and KFOR.

UNMIK's Legal Department hurriedly drafted Regulation 26/1999, which extends the time for preindictment detention to a maximum of one year for offenses carrying a minimum prison sentence of five years, and the "proper administration of justice" demands that this extension occur. A judge or the public prosecutor must issue a reasoned decision justifying the extension order.

The Human Rights Office of the SRSG had several problems with the regulation because it violated international human rights standards, and the office provided a detailed memorandum expressing its concerns and a possible solution. In particular, the period of one year before indictment contradicts Article 9(3) of the International Covenant on Civil and Political Rights and Article 5(3) of the European Convention for the Protection of Human Rights and Fundamental Freedoms. Our concern was with the length of the detention period and the failure to provide a mechanism by which to challenge the detention order in an open, adversarial hearing. There was no possibility to review this decision to prolong detention. While we agreed that more time was needed and that Kosovo faced a judicial vacuum and an ongoing conflict, the means chosen in Regulation 26 were deeply flawed.

We recommended that the UN recognize the extraordinary nature of the situation in Kosovo and declare a temporary derogation from Article 9 of the covenant as allowed by Article 4. The SRSG's Human Rights Office argued that Kosovo presented exactly the conditions contemplated for suspension of treaty obligations until a "public emergency" had ended. The time limit for detentions could be extended and a procedure for a regular review of the ongoing detention created. We did not succeed; it appears that UNMIK did not want to admit that Kosovo was a public emergency when regular reports to UN headquarters emphasized how well everything was progressing. As expected, UNMIK came in for heavy criticism of Regulation 26 by the OSCE's Legal Systems Monitoring Section (LSMS) and by Amnesty International.

This detention problem illustrates the tension inherent in modern UN trusteeship-type operations. UN missions like UNMIK, with assistance from KFOR, are responsible for law and order in situations where conflict continues or is barely contained. Yet an extensive regime of international human rights guarantees has evolved since the last time the UN was deeply involved in the trusteeship business. Squaring its obligations to uphold human rights with providing security is a central tension in Kosovo. UNMIK has not always acquitted itself well, as evidenced in Regulation 26. UNMIK also drew criticism by giving itself immunity from the new Ombudsperson's jurisdiction in Regulation 38/2000 (June 30, 2000). This set a bad example for local government officials by allowing diplomatic privileges and immunities granted to UNMIK international personnel to trump the jurisdiction of the Office of the Ombudsperson, the new governmental organ responsible for ensuring compliance with international human rights standards. Ombudsperson Marek Novicki ordered SRSG Haekkerup to amend UNMIK regulations by removing this immunity for UNMIK employees.[9]

To avoid future problems, the UN should include in the legal departments of these missions, which are effectively legislatures, a human rights expert who can vet the draft regulations to ensure compliance with human rights standards so that mistakes like those found in Regulation 26 are caught and corrected early.

APPLICABLE LAW DISPUTE

The UN made a decision in July 1999 that had a major impact on the judiciary and on its own credibility. A fundamental question had to be answered: what law would apply in Kosovo now that UNMIK and NATO were in charge of administering the territory? In its very first regulation, UNMIK decided that the law in force on March 23, 1999 (the day before the start of the NATO air campaign) would apply as long as this law was consistent with international human rights law and Security Council Resolution 1244.[10]

The Albanian-dominated judiciary rejected this decision, saying publicly that they would not apply "Serbian" law in Kosovo. They agreed to apply federal law, such as the Yugoslav federal code of criminal procedure, but they would not apply the Serbian penal code covering substantive criminal law that was in force in Kosovo on the specified date. The Albanians insisted on applying the Kosovo criminal code and other provincial laws that were in effect in March 1989 when the Belgrade authorities illegally stripped Kosovo of its autonomy and made it an integral part of the Serb Republic.

UNMIK's decision led to civil disobedience among the Albanian judiciary. They simply refused to apply the 1999 law and thus flagrantly violated UNMIK Regulation 1. All criminal trials held in Kosovo during the period August–December 1999 applied the Kosovo criminal code and the Yugoslav code of criminal procedure. Although the Serb and Kosovo codes do not differ much, the failure to apply the requisite law created both legal and political uncertainty. The legal validity of every case decided under a law that should not have been applied was in doubt. Moreover, the likelihood of convincing the Serb jurists to return to the judiciary fell to zero because they would never agree to implement the Kosovo code of 1989, which they regarded as a "retrograde, communist law." The application of the wrong law also created great confusion among the UN CIVPOL, whose members came from more than forty countries; they struggled gamely with trying to understand what law they should apply in making arrests, conducting searches and seizures, and questioning suspects. The unsettled legal situation made their already difficult job only more challenging.

The credibility of the judiciary was further jeopardized when Albanian judges "borrowed" from the 1999 law in cases involving drug trafficking and war crimes, because the Kosovo 1989 code did not contain any provisions covering these acts. In private, Albanian lawyers admitted that the 1999 law was superior in many respects but that as a political matter they could not possibly apply any law with "Serbia" in its title.

This dispute spread even to the new Kosovo police school. The director of the school had contracted with six local lawyers to teach basic criminal law to the new Kosovo police cadets. The lawyers, all Albanians, refused to teach the 1999 law and insisted on teaching the 1989 Kosovo code. The school director, taking a position unusual for a senior UNMIK official at this point, refused to bend and told the lawyers that they either had to teach the applicable law based on UNMIK Regulation 1 or be fired. They refused, so the director fired them.

The uncertainty dragged on. Yet as early as September 1999, several UNMIK officers, supported by KFOR lawyers, urged that the UN simply take a model penal code, change the name, and declare it to be the provisional applicable criminal statute for Kosovo; in the meantime, experts from the Council of Europe could complete an overhaul of the existing Kosovo code. This idea was not accepted, and in December 1999, the UN relented and reversed itself on the applicable law question. In Regulation 24/1999, UNMIK declared that the laws in effect on March 22, 1989, would be the applicable law in Kosovo.[11] This decision only made the UN look weak in the eyes of many and demoralized many staff members and the CIVPOL.

The Kosovo situation provides a case study to support the Brahimi peacekeeping panel's recommendation that in such situations the UN should avoid entangling political and legal issues by imposing a generic penal code and code of criminal procedure with modern human rights guarantees for an interim period.[12] This code should include a provision allowing for habeas corpus challenges to detention orders. The Kosovo experience amply supports also the Brahimi panel's recommendation that fully staffed "emergency judicial teams," to include judges, prosecutors, defense counsel, human rights lawyers, and experts on detention and detainee rights, should also be part of any initial peacekeeping deployment. One KFOR district commander said, "We should have sent in lawyers, judges and police to take control right away and impose exceptional laws if this is what is necessary."

UNMIK'S RESPONSE TO THE LOGISTICAL PROBLEMS

UNMIK's greatest success in the judicial reform area was its response to the absence of the basic materials necessary for a court system to work. In 2000, UNMIK's Administrative Department of Judicial Affairs (ADJ) completed an inventory of the courts and prosecutors' offices to highlight their needs.[13]

The ADJ had limited resources so it scrambled to identify donors to support its efforts to equip the judiciary. The U.S. Department of State was particularly helpful, donating $2.5 million for computers, printers, vehicles, typewriters, and photocopiers. In all, the ADJ, according to its records, provided "32 vehicles, 502 desks, 984 chairs, 374 bookcases, 58 computers, 15 photocopiers, 200 typewriters, 150 filing cabinets and 5 generators, as well as court stamps, ID cards, and legal forms."[14] Thirty buildings were rehabilitated, thanks largely to funds from the U.K. This is a significant achievement in a postconflict situation; I have worked in several other UN missions where the physical need to rebuild the judiciary was as pressing, and I have never seen quicker results.

TRANSITION FROM THE EMERGENCY JUDICIAL SYSTEM

UNMIK's Emergency Judicial System functioned from June to December 1999. Judges and prosecutors received three-month renewable contracts. After an initial flurry of appointments, the system focused on pretrial detentions and investigation of criminal complaints. The Kosovo judiciary requires lay judges for criminal trials in district courts (where the possible sentence is greater than five years), and UNMIK found it difficult to identify and recruit them in sufficient numbers in the early days. The district court in Prizren was the only one to conduct criminal trials in the emergency phase because it recruited lay judges.

Another recurring problem in the emergency phase was the poor pay offered to judges, prosecutors, and support staff. In fact, UNMIK could not offer salaries in the first months; UNMIK paid an initial "stipend" of 500 deutsche mark (DM) in August followed by monthly stipends of DM 300 for judges and prosecutors. By comparison, UNMIK drivers and interpreters, often much younger and less experienced than judges and prosecutors, earned at least twice as much. Court workers in Pristina went on strike in October 1999 to protest the low salaries. Yet budget realities could not be ignored: Kosovo has limited revenue-raising capacity, and other public salaries are also low; it would not be helpful to inflate salaries that could not be maintained. This must be weighed against the potential for corruption and the difficulty in attracting and retaining qualified and talented staff.

Starting in November 1999, the ADJ began interviewing candidates for the next phase after the termination of the Emergency Judicial System. ADJ staff interviewed hundreds of people all over Kosovo, sometimes as many as two dozen in a day. Most had worked in the judiciary prior to the 1989 loss of autonomy. The regular judicial system began working in January 2000, first in Gnjilane where, on January 18, thirty-six judges and four public prosecutors took the oath of office. Similar ceremonies occurred in the other four district courts over the next six weeks.

By September 2000, UNMIK had recruited 405 judges and prosecutors and 724 support staff for all the courts in Kosovo. The goal is to reach a total of 1,665 positions.[15] This would be sufficient to meet the needs of a population of about 2 million based on comparative European standards.

While UNMIK, in a short amount of time and with minimal resources and planning, has accomplished a great deal toward establishing a court system, two key and related problems persist and inhibit efforts to create the rule of law. First, security for all those working in the system is precarious, especially for the few minority participants. Second, the instances of bias and intimidation, combined with a lack of knowledge or will to impose certain human rights guarantees, has led to flawed judicial proceedings and unjust results.

SECURITY FOR THE JUDICIARY

Given the overall insecurity in Kosovo, it should be no surprise that judges and prosecutors frequently are afraid. Since they are charged with investigating, prosecuting, and convicting people in cases where criminal enterprises, ethnic allegiance, and great amounts of money are often at issue, the judiciary is particularly vulnerable. KFOR and UNMIK police are already stretched thin by crime, ethnic violence, an insurgency in southeastern Kosovo by an offshoot of the UCK that wants to annex the Presevo Valley of southern Serbia to Kosovo, and an insurgency along the Kosovo-Macedonian border that has drawn U.S. KFOR into firefights with the Albanian insurgents.[16]

UNMIK officials admit that security is a major problem, asserting that KFOR and UN CIVPOL refuse to assign staff to guard the courts.[17] The new Kosovo Police Service is supposed to provide court security, but they too are understaffed. There has been at least one incident of a threat made in open court by a former UCK officer against a judge in Pec.[18] The head prosecutor in Pec revealed that he has been threatened.[19] And in another case in the Pec region, one judge asked that a case involving a high-ranking former UCK member be removed from his docket because it was too "dangerous." This judge feared for his life and the lives of his family. No judge in the district wanted this case; the detainee had been in prison since May 2000 awaiting an international judge to take up the case. A Serb noted that "for the moment, even if a judge wants to act impartially, the population puts too much pressure on the judge and he can't act properly."[20]

Instances of judges being verbally threatened in their own courthouses by unknown individuals have occurred in several Kosovo towns. In one case, Albanian judges threatened a Muslim Slav colleague in Pristina because she insisted on holding hearings in Bosnian. The security situation for Albanian judges in Serb-dominated northern Mitrovica, where the district court is located, is horrible, but at least here, by force of circumstance, KFOR and UN police provide constant security. OSCE human rights officers for several months provided daily transport from the south to the north and then home again for the Albanian judges.

A policy covering transporting prisoners to court also needs to be elaborated. For example, the Italian Carabinieri, who are part of KFOR, insist that this is not their job; CIVPOL have also stated that this is not in their mandate. So sometimes prisoners do not reach court for appointed hearings. In one case, a detainee in Dragash went on a hunger strike because he had missed three court dates due to lack of transport.[21]

KFOR and UNMIK must design a comprehensive security policy for all courthouses and prosecutors' offices so that they may work in safe and secure surroundings. It will be impossible to attract minority participants otherwise, thus ensuring that Kosovo's judiciary remains monoethnic.

BIAS AND UNFAIRNESS

Bias affects the course of justice in two ways. First, cases involving minority defendants in criminal proceedings present real challenges to administer justice fairly. Second, cases involving former UCK or other powerful Albanians or those with powerful connections are also ripe for abuse.

All the problems discussed earlier about the presumption of collective guilt and the intense polarization encouraged by extremists on both sides get magnified in the judiciary. This is especially true given the monoethnic character of Kosovo's judiciary, where few judges and prosecutors are from minority groups and only a handful are Serbs. The reality is that a Serb defendant, who most likely has an Albanian defense lawyer, faces an Albanian judge, Albanian lay judges, and an Albanian prosecutor. Independent Albanian analysts admit that it is very difficult for a Serb to get a fair trial in Kosovo without the participation of international jurists.

At one point, over thirty Serbs were in detention on charges of genocide, war crimes, and crimes against humanity. In August 2000, about fourteen of them escaped from the detention center in northern Mitrovica, which was being guarded by UNMIK police.[22] But for the rest, trial in Kosovo courts awaits.

Instances of bias against Serbs and other minorities among the Albanian judiciary surfaced early during the Emergency Judicial System and have continued ever since. U.S. Army lawyers and their British colleagues reported cases of racist statements made in open court about Serbs. Several UCK members visited a judge and prosecutor who were working in the Camp Bondsteel detention facility, and five UCK in detention were ordered released immediately. In another case, an Albanian judge was heard to say about a Serb, "He has an accent like the one who killed my family, so let's convict him."[23] When pressed, some Albanian judges have admitted that they decide cases differently, even apply different sections of the penal code, in cases involving Serbs.

Albanians arrested on serious charges, often caught red-handed by KFOR or UNMIK police, frequently were released immediately or were not indicted and subsequently released. Meanwhile, Serbs, Roma, and other minorities arrested on even minor charges with flimsy evidence were almost always detained, and some stayed in detention even though they were not indicted. This frustrated and demoralized KFOR and UNMIK police. One KFOR officer said the impunity enjoyed by Albanians in the Klina area shocked all his peers; one local frequently boasted that he could beat and steal whenever he wanted because the judiciary would release him anyway. "I don't know what it would take to arrest and detain an Albanian, it would take some imagination to envision this," said another KFOR soldier. A CIVPOL officer with more than a year's experience in Kosovo spoke for many of his exasperated fellow officers when he said, "When I arrest an Albanian, I always complete my report within 72 hours and present it to the judge, but the person is almost always released. I'm tired of wasting my time. I prepared a complete report on arson on a Serb house,

but the prosecutor released the suspect immediately. Only here is possession of a hand grenade considered a minor offense."[24]

To counter bias against Serbs, several UNMIK police admitted that
they would not arrest Serbs unless the offense was very serious; otherwise
they knew the Serb would be detained for a long time even for a minor
offense. In one case, a Kosovo Serb was arrested and detained on the basis
of dubious statements made by three witnesses whose testimony was incon-
sistent. Nevertheless, the Albanian prosecutor decided that the investigation
should continue, and the suspect remained in detention.[25] In another case, a
Serb was arrested and six people said he was a war criminal, yet they could
not identify him as the person alleged to have committed a crime.[26] Cases
involving illegal possession of arms are another fertile ground for discriminatory treatment. In Mitrovica, Serbs charged with this offense have faced
long and unreasonable delays in the investigations; some have been in
detention for months pending an investigation even though the maximum
sentence for this offense is twelve months.

Meanwhile, most Albanians charged with the same offense are released
immediately. This holds true for other criminal charges where solid evidence against Albanians resulted in their quick release even before an
investigation was completed. For example, an Albanian arrested in connection with the kidnapping and disappearance of two Serb schoolteachers
who visited the education office in Urosevac/Ferizaj in August 1999 was
released on the order of a three-judge panel despite strong circumstantial
evidence presented to the investigating judge.[27] The teachers have never
been found despite the KFOR commander's promise to the families to find
them. In Gnjilane, in October 1999, an investigating judge ordered the
release of two Albanians who had admitted that they attempted to murder
someone they believed was a Serb. The judge said he had received a note
from the prosecutor ordering their release; KFOR refused to allow the
release saying that they could not honor an order issued by the prosecutor
in this way, which they deemed not official.[28] In Pristina District Court, on
October 27, 1999, a seventy-seven-year-old Serb male identified his attackers and kidnappers, two young Albanians. A medical exam confirmed he
had received serious injuries. Nevertheless, the prosecutor found the victim's testimony not credible, refusing to believe that a Kosovo Serb could
"walk the streets," and rejected the victim's testimony as "unreliable."[29] In
Prizren, in November 1999, a former UCK member charged with raping a
Gorani woman was released because the investigating judge lost the case
file. When Kosovo Serb Orthodox priests were shot and wounded in Klokot
in June 2000, the Albanian judge quickly released the main Albanian suspect whom CIVPOL had arrested. The Lawyers Committee for Human
Rights, a respected international NGO, published a report in October 1999
expressing alarm at the high level of releases of detainees arrested for seri-

ous crimes where CIVPOL either had caught the suspect red-handed or had very strong incriminating evidence.[30]

In several cases where the court has ordered Albanians released even though there was strong incriminating evidence against them, the KFOR commander has overruled the court's decision and ordered the suspect to remain in detention. The commander based his decision on UN Security Council Resolution 1244 requiring NATO to provide security in Kosovo; the commander reasoned that releasing the suspect would compromise security. These cases have usually involved suspects who have directly threatened or endangered KFOR personnel. While the goal of the decision was understandable and overall security was probably enhanced, the means chosen by Commander KFOR undermined the rule of law in Kosovo. This was not the proper way to combat ethnic bias or intimidation in the courts. What the KFOR commander should have done was to issue a reasoned decision explaining why he was overruling the judiciary and allow lawyers for the suspect to challenge or rebut the decision. A panel of judicial experts, a majority international with some local members, could then have reviewed the decision.

Equally controversial was the decision of SRSG Kouchner to order the ongoing detention of Afrim Zeqiri, an Albanian and former UCK fighter, arrested on suspicion of murdering three Serbs on May 28, 2000, in the village of Cernica. The crime was especially despicable because one of those shot and killed was a four-year-old boy. An Albanian prosecutor ordered the suspect released for lack of evidence, arousing the usual suspicions of judicial bias, but this decision was confirmed by an international judge. The SRSG's "executive hold" extending detention was based on "security reasons" and the authority under Security Council Resolution 1244. The decision to overrule the international judge generated a storm of criticism from the OSCE Legal System Monitoring Section and from international human rights groups. The European Magistrates for Democracy and Liberties expressed "extreme concern," noting that "the detention authorization you gave to KFOR . . . is of a nature to ruin the credibility of Kosovar justice . . . peace in Kosovo can come only through the rule of law."[31] Zeqiri's lawyer wrote a letter to Kouchner demanding his client's immediate release, citing provisions in the European human rights convention outlawing illegal arrest and detention. The lawyer also noted that the SRSG's decision gives rise to "suspicion . . . in the work of the Court system."[32] Zeqiri's trial is expected to begin in the fall of 2001; motions challenging his indictment and extending his detention were heard by a panel of international judges in July 2001. Defense lawyers also tried to have the international prosecutor removed from the case.

Security is a major concern in Kosovo, and there are violent people willing to murder to advance their agendas. The SRSG and KFOR commander have difficult challenges in preserving a minimal level of security. Yet ruling by fiat without giving detailed reasons and with no opportunity to challenge or review these detention decisions is not the way to encourage respect for the rule of law and an independent judiciary, no matter how reasonable the goal. The judiciary in communist and postcommunist Kosovo had been thoroughly politicized; this tradition and the mind-set that goes with it must be broken. UNMIK must create an independent judiciary free from political interference. On August 25, 2001, the SRSG signed Regulation 18/2001, which addresses the problems of extra-judicial detentions based on executive orders. The regulation creates a three-person panel of internationals who will review detentions based on executive orders. The panel will either confirm or overturn the executive order and its decision is final.

Despite so many clear cases of judicial and prosecutorial bias and incompetence, UNMIK did not remove, warn, or discipline a single judge. The Advisory Judicial Commission, established to oversee the judiciary, "is a complete disaster," according to one senior UN official, and was dissolved in October 2000. It was replaced by a Kosovo Judicial and Prosecutorial Council, which includes international jurists with experience from Bosnia. Without a serious disciplinary mechanism, judges and prosecutors enjoy impunity themselves with pernicious effects on the actual and perceived state of justice.

One of the most egregious cases of ethnic bias in the courts involved the Momcilovic family, ethnic Serbs living in Gnjilane. Thanks to a videotape from a security camera that was running over the entry to the Momcilovic home and auto supply shop, the facts are clear.[33] On July 10, 1999, at about five P.M., four Albanian men armed with handguns approached the home. They started to shout the names of the Momcilovic men and urged them to come out. One of the men started kicking the door of the house, trying to open it. A shot was fired, apparently from the house where the Momcilovic family was ensconced. The four men were not harmed and they started shooting at the house. Then heavy gunfire, including automatic weapons, was heard, followed by exchange of fire between U.S. Army snipers, who had taken up positions on top of a nearby building, and the four men.[34]

The firefight between the U.S. troops and the four men resulted in two Albanians killed and two injured. One of those killed was a purported UCK "war hero," Afrim Gagice. KFOR arrested all three Momcilovic males who were in the house, along with the two wounded Albanians. All were taken to Camp Bondsteel, the main U.S. military base in Kosovo, which contains a detention center.

The prosecution indicted the three Momcilovic men for murder and attempted murder on January 7, 2000. One of the surviving Albanians was indicted for attempted murder of U.S. soldiers but was released in December 1999; he was never charged with the attack on the Momcilovics. The other survivor was never charged with any crime.

The existence of the videotape became known as early as October 1999 when U.S. military lawyers informed the OSCE of its existence. The investigating judge and prosecutor also knew about it but never viewed it. It is extraordinary to say the least that the judicial officials responsible for drafting the indictment of the Momcilovics did not even seem interested in viewing the video. Even worse, when a new prosecutor was named, he did view the tape (in April 2000) and "saw nothing."[35] Yet this did not stop him from trying to exclude the introduction of the video from trial. Also, surprisingly, the UN Administrative Department of Judicial Affairs supported excluding the video from trial.[36]

Any fair-minded person viewing the video would have never indicted the Momcilovic men and would have indicted the surviving armed attackers; in fact, the precise opposite occurred. The video supports the Momcilovic's contention that they acted in self-defense and contradicts sworn testimony by the Albanian defendants that they were not armed. The Momcilovics spent more than a year in prison for crimes they never committed.

A first trial began on April 25, 2000, but was adjourned. The trial panel comprised five local judges (two professional, three lay). Both the prosecutor and defense counsel requested to submit additional evidence. The second trial started in July and ended in August; this time an international judge participated in the panel. The video was finally shown in open court on July 20. Moreover, the statements of a U.S. soldier from an official army investigation of the incident were entered into the court record. This testimony showed beyond a reasonable doubt that U.S. soldiers had killed two of the Albanians, thus completely exonerating the Momcilovics of the most serious charges.[37] Yet the trial went on, even though the evidence now pointed the other way. If it had not been for the intense international scrutiny raised by the press and the participation of an international judge, the result in this case might well have been a conviction. As a final insult, the court convicted the Momcilovics of "illegal weapons possession" and sentenced them to twelve months, a wildly excessive sentence compared to similar cases involving Albanian defendants. Fortunately, the Momcilovics had already served more than twelve months so they were finally released at the trial's conclusion, receiving credit for time served.

INTERNATIONAL PARTICIPATION IN THE JUDICIARY

Several UNMIK officials working on judicial reform became convinced that international judges and prosecutors had to participate in trials involving ethnic violence, war crimes, crimes against humanity, and serious crimes implicating criminal syndicates. Otherwise, the whole effort to build an independent judiciary would fail. While routine criminal matters and most civil cases could and should be left to the Kosovo jurists, evidence of intimidation and bias in serious cases was overwhelming.[38] If the new Kosovo Police Service needed constant international oversight and mentoring, wasn't it just as apparent and necessary that the equally sensitive work of prosecuting and judging high-profile cases would require international participation and oversight?

The first calls for international jurists were made in a series of internal UNMIK meetings as early as September 1999. As cases like Momcilovic became known and more common, this need became more apparent. Yet there was resistance within UNMIK at the highest levels. At one point, a senior UN official responded to the recommendation by saying, "This is not the Congo you know." Aside from the racial bias revealed by this response, it showed the undue depth of deference accorded by some UNMIK officials to the local power structure dominated by Albanian hard-liners and a lack of understanding about how ethnic bias affected the judiciary. Some UNMIK officials were afraid of "offending" the Albanians by taking a step that so clearly showed a lack of confidence in their ability or desire to administer justice fairly. Another UNMIK official demanded hard proof of instances of ethnic bias, yet even when informed of the ongoing Momcilovic travesty and other similar examples, UNMIK's position remained unchanged.

UNMIK's attitude toward international participation in the judiciary changed in February 2000. On February 4, a vicious attack occurred near the Serb village of Banja, west of Mitrovica. A UNHCR bus with about forty Serbs on board was returning from Mitrovica, where people on board had done various shopping, banking, mailing, and other errands impossible to do in their isolated enclaves. The bus was escorted by French KFOR, who had placed armored personnel carriers in front and behind the bus. As the bus slowed to almost a complete stop to negotiate a hairpin turn in the road, someone fired a rocket from a nearby hill. The rocket hit the bus but fortunately did not explode. Two people were killed by the impact. The bus contained mostly old-age pensioners and young children. French KFOR attempted to apprehend the attackers, but the fields between the road and the hill were heavily mined; the attackers escaped and have never been caught. This was obviously a carefully planned attack.

Outrage mounted swiftly at this attack, which was carried out with military precision requiring experience with rocket launchers, not the usual weapon of common criminals. Northern Mitrovica exploded a few days later in violence when at least eight people, mostly Albanians and a few identified as Turks, were killed by Serb extremists. Hundreds of Albanians fled from the north. According to well-informed OSCE officers, the TMK was at the same time ordering Albanians to leave Mitrovica and was attempting to infiltrate its members to take their place.[39] Albanians hijacked an ambulance from an Italian NGO in southern Kosovo and then filled it with weapons and ammunition. This bold attempt to abuse the sanctity given to medical vehicles did not succeed when the ambulance ran off the road as it approached a KFOR checkpoint on the southern approach to Mitrovica. Soon, in the north, CIVPOL and KFOR arrested known TMK members with TMK identity cards. They and other Albanians were released almost immediately by the local judiciary, also Albanian, despite eyewitness testimony that they were shooting at KFOR and Serb apartments. The KFOR French commander in Mitrovica not surprisingly was enraged and demanded that UNMIK take action, since people who had shot at his soldiers that morning were back on the street hours after arrest.

Overnight, the UNMIK Legal Department, which often took months to issue the simplest regulation, presented Regulation 6/2000 for SRSG Kouchner's signature. This regulation allows for international judges and prosecutors to be appointed to the district court in Mitrovica as an emergency measure. It was finally clear that without international participation, the judiciary could not operate freely and fairly, thus jeopardizing the security situation in Kosovo. This lesson took much too long to learn and is a principal reason why armed extremists on both sides continue to operate freely. "There was too much optimism," one senior UNMIK official admitted. "We thought 'Let's appoint some judges, some good people, they have their freedom and they will be good and behave properly.'" This was naïve and showed a fundamental misunderstanding of Kosovo. Even after the events of February 2000 in Mitrovica, some in UNMIK and in the ADJ opposed introducing international judges and prosecutors. Unfortunately, as with most things in life, it is much easier to deal with a problem early than late.

Several months later, UNMIK passed Regulation 34/2000 extending the authorization to appoint international judges and prosecutors to every district court in Kosovo. By October 2000, international judges and prosecutors worked in every district court in Kosovo. According to the then co-head of the Department of Justice, Sylvie Pantz, the local judges, after some initial resentment about the higher salaries, "are accepting the internationals, the internationals are having a positive impact."[40] In serving as informal mentors, these international jurists provide on-the-job advice and by their work give positive examples of how to administer justice without bias. Unfortunately, reflecting the reality of Kosovo, these international judges require heavy security protection as they investigate and prosecute powerful people. This only underscores how unlikely and even unfair it is to ask local judges for now to handle such cases.

While the appointment of international judges was long overdue, it is no panacea. Some international judges are afraid; one of them admitted to an OSCE Legal Systems Monitoring officer that he was afraid to investigate a trafficking-in-women case because it is so "sensitive."[41]

Moreover, UN administrators have also hindered investigations against high-profile Albanians. In one case, CIVPOL had discovered and confirmed an illegal tax scheme that led directly to Hacim Thaci's inner circle. Yet, according to the CIVPOL officer in charge of the investigation, senior UNMIK officials refused to allow the police to arrest the suspects. A Swedish judge, Christer Karphammar, who worked for eighteen months in Kosovo as a prosecutor and then judge, said he "directly knows of several cases in which UN and KFOR senior officials opposed or blocked prosecution of former Kosovo Liberation Army members, including some now in the KPC [TMK]. . . The investigations were stopped on a high level," and for the entire time he worked in Kosovo "the judiciary was not allowed to work independently."[42]

A SPECIALIZED TRIBUNAL FOR KOSOVO?

Kosovo Serbs and several other minority detainees in Mitrovica started a hunger strike in April 2000 to protest the release of an Albanian alleged to have thrown a grenade in a crowd, the slowness of their own case investigations, and bias in the courts. Most had been arrested more than six months before and still had not been indicted. Yet rushing their trials, which involve complex issues, is also fraught with danger. War crimes and genocide are sensitive and complicated issues that mature judicial systems expend great time and resources adjudicating. It is unrealistic to expect the nascent Kosovo system, short of resources and experience and widely perceived as biased against Serbs and other minorities, to handle these cases.

A proposed Kosovo War and Ethnic Crimes Court (KWECC) was briefly floated to respond to this need. This would have been a domestic tribunal with jurisdiction over war crimes, serious violations of international humanitarian law, and serious ethnically motivated crimes. It was to have local and international judging panels and an appellate tribunal. One problem was that each panel was to have two local and one international judge, so that the locals still would have been able to outvote the international. An Office of the Defense, which would include local and international lawyers, was also to be established to provide defense counsel to the accused.

After facing numerous delays in its implementing regulation—with numerous drafts flying back and forth between Pristina and UN headquarters in New York—and funding difficulties, UNMIK announced on September 11, 2000, that the KWECC proposal was dead. Yet at least seventeen cases, with more on the way, were within the proposed KWECC's jurisdiction as of September 2000; they now would be handled by the normal Kosovo justice system, with all its problems. The first genocide trial in Kosovo began in December 2000 with an international prosecutor and one international judge on a five-person panel consisting entirely of Albanians. The defendant was Serb.

Following a crescendo of criticism and concern about the bias in the judiciary, UNMIK passed Regulation 64/2000 on December 15, 2000. This regulation finally recognized what several people in UNMIK had been saying for more than a year: "that the presence of security threats may undermine the independence and impartiality of the judiciary and impede the ability of the judiciary to properly prosecute crimes which gravely undermine the peace process and the full establishment of the rule of law in Kosovo." The regulation provides that the prosecutor, the accused, or the defense counsel may at any time during criminal proceedings petition the ADJ to assign international judges or prosecutors or to change the venue of the proceedings "to ensure the independence and impartiality of the judiciary or the proper administration of justice." The final decision rests with the SRSG. If a judicial panel is appointed, at least two of its three members must be international judges.

Yet even the presence of international jurists does not preclude the appearance of bias and possible interference with the judiciary. In a case attracting international attention, a three-judge panel, including two internationals, found Zoran Stanojevic, a thirty-five-year-old former Serb policeman, guilty of taking part in the January 1999 Racak massacre. Amnesty International and some UN legal officers involved in the case criticized the trial and the verdict, noting that it was "dogged by procedural irregularities and that trial testimony was contradicted by forensic evidence and initial witness statements.[43] The lawyer representing the victims' families in the case even threatened the court, stating that the families will have to seek revenge if there were an acquittal. A UN official stated the judges "gave in to pressure, pressure that was exerted throughout the case."[44] A UN spokesperson and one of the judges involved in the case strenuously denied the accusations of intimidation and procedural flaws.

OSCE SIX-MONTH REPORT

The OSCE's Legal Systems Monitoring Section of the Human Rights Division had monitored the performance of the Kosovo justice system. This caused some discomfort among those in Pillar Two of UNMIK, especially the ADJ, responsible for civil administration. Having one pillar—the OSCE, responsible for institutional development—assess and criticize in public the performance of another pillar was unusual. Tension between the two flared upon the release in October 2000 of the OSCE's report on the justice system, *Kosovo: A Review of the Criminal Justice System 1 February 2000 – 31 July 2000.*

This ninety-page report examines the judiciary's performance in the period between February 1 and July 31, 2000, the first six months following the period of the Emergency Judicial System, which ended in January 2000. The report is comprehensive and hard-hitting and provides numerous examples to illustrate deficiencies previously identified. It makes dozens of recommendations while recognizing the complexity of UNMIK's task of creating an entire justice system from scratch.

After an initial adverse reaction to the report, UN officials stopped acting defensively and realized the report was not a personal attack on their competence or commitment. The UN and OSCE formed working groups to tackle the myriad problems highlighted in the report. Unfortunately, the working groups have made little progress to date in implementing the report's recommendations.

The OSCE monitored seventy-seven of the 116 district court criminal trials completed during the period covered by the report. LSMS monitors also attended pretrial hearings; visited detention centers, spoke with judges, prosecutors, defense counsel, police, and prison officials; and reviewed case files. The report puts flesh and bones on the problems faced in administering justice, provides statistics, spots trends, and also recognizes areas of improvement. Among the crucial problems detailed at length with numerous examples in the report are:

• Few lawyers and judges have a working knowledge of international human rights law. In all the cases monitored by the OSCE, in only two instances was international human rights law invoked; the concept of "equality of arms" is unknown and great deference is shown to the prosecution, undoubtedly a legacy of the forty years of communist law, which unfortunately is the only experience most of those working in the current system have.

• Access to defense counsel is difficult for minorities. In northern Mitrovica, Kosovo Serb lawyers are not permitted to meet with their clients before the first detention hearing and thereafter are not permitted confidential communications with their client; they must obtain prior written "permission" from the investigating judge.

• Defense counsel are largely passive, rarely cross-examining witnesses or introducing evidence. Defense counsel rarely challenge court orders, including detention and extension of detention. Local law provides for an active role by defense counsel at all stages of criminal proceedings, yet few fulfill this role. Defense counsel fail to request forensic evidence, fail to object at trial to inadmissible evidence, and fail to question adequately all witnesses.

• Lengthy pretrial and precharge detentions continue, with some detainees not brought before a judge within twenty-four hours of arrest as required under applicable Yugoslav law (which can be extended to seventy-two hours in exceptional cases, though even this latter period is often not respected). Kosovo Serbs, including a few juveniles, have been disproportionately affected by lengthy pretrial detention, in some cases exceeding one year.

• FRY criminal procedure law fails to provide for immediate access to defense counsel in violation of international human rights law; this right is also violated in practice.

• Many pretrial detention decisions fail to state the precise facts justifying the detention; most merely repeat the wording of the FRY statute.

• There is currently no habeas corpus mechanism in the Kosovo judicial process to challenge the lawfulness of an arrest or detention.

• Of 196 defendants interviewed by the OSCE in all five district courts, "none reported that they had access to defense counsel whilst in detention prior to the first detention hearing."[45] This lack of access largely stems from the absence of a mechanism by which to appoint or authorize representation by defense counsel.

• Defendants report that on the rare occasions that their counsel comes to meet with them prior to trial, those visits are extremely brief and usually occur right before the trial, indicating that the time and effort to prepare an adequate defense is lacking.

• Defense counsel has limited access to prosecution files; police reports are off-limits in most cases, thus inhibiting the defense preparation of the case.

• Pay for court-appointed lawyers is very low so that most refuse to take these cases, making obtaining representation for criminal defendants more difficult.

• The Kosovo justice system is widely viewed as lacking impartiality; this view is based on both objective and subjective factors.

• Discriminatory treatment is especially prevalent in decisions regarding pretrial detention; Albanians are routinely released regardless of the evidence, while Serbs are detained.

• The courts are reluctant to prosecute cases of sexual violence, especially if the alleged victim is from a minority group. The legal system lacks expertise in this area, and safe houses, counseling/treatment, court advocates representing the victim's interests, and security for victims of sexual violence are inadequate or nonexistent. The extent of sexual violence in Kosovo, as in many societies, is vastly underreported and not acknowledged.

The OSCE report concludes by acknowledging that the UN had to start from scratch, in a situation of ongoing conflict, to mount a justice system that also would have to adjudicate complex and serious cases that challenge the most sophisticated legal systems and practitioners: genocide, war crimes, and crimes against humanity. Despite great effort and commitment,

> There still exist significant gaps between the required logistical capacity of the courts, the experience and competence of the relevant actors, and the reality on the ground. Whilst a focus of attention has been on the treatment of minorities in the justice system, the gaps in the existing system have impacted upon all individuals, including the victims and witness[es].[46]

Six months after the October 2000 report, the LSMS issued an update.[47] It found that most of the shortcomings identified previously persisted. Judges still failed to apply international human rights law, showing that the training held on the applicable law issue was deficient. The absence of an effective habeas corpus mechanism remains a major human rights problem as does continuing restrictions on suspects' access to counsel. This latter human rights violation was highlighted more than a year ago. Judges continue to apply a section of the FRY criminal procedure code that violates human rights principles because it restricts the defendant's ability to prepare a defense, and defense lawyers remain passive. Sound legal reasoning and skillful use of evidence are uncommon. On the positive side, the OSCE had created and distributed a desk reference for defense counsel on criminal procedure, and the ADJ of UNMIK had strengthened the judicial inspection unit.

The problem is that in the case of Kosovo, as in East Timor, the UN is directly responsible for administering justice. Neither the OSCE nor the UN can just sit back and criticize "the authorities" for bias or failure to comply with international standards; the UN is the state and must guarantee fair trials, access to counsel, laws that comply with international human rights, and utter fairness. UNMIK must take steps to address the shortcomings identified, which include removing judges and prosecutors who exhibit bias. UNMIK must devote more resources to the courts; training must be greatly improved and based on the practical challenges of Kosovo and not on theoretical niceties more suitable to a law school seminar in Strasbourg. Young jurists, untainted by the previous system, need to be recruited on an urgent basis and offered a decent salary and career prospects. The UN and OSCE must identify, train, and support criminal defense attorneys so that they can represent the accused vigorously and make the prosecution prove its case, a revolution in Kosovo's legal tradition.

Without a free and fair judiciary, given the political and security climate, violence will persist, threatening the chances of success of other UNMIK and KFOR initiatives, especially the international police and the new Kosovo Police Service.

NOTES

1. International Covenant on Civil and Political Rights, Article 4, defines which rights can be suspended ("derogated") during a "time of public emergency which threatens the life of the nation and the existence of which is officially proclaimed."

2. Interview, Pristina, September 21, 2000.

3. A similar phenomenon occurred in Bosnia, where General Clark notes, "the more we pushed the hard-line Serbs, the less they wanted to challenge us." *Waging Modern War* (New York: Public Affairs, 2001) p. 105.

4. For a discussion of INTERFET's interim legal regime, see Major Bruce M. Oswald, "INTERFET Detainee Management Unit in East Timor" (undated draft on file with the author).

5. UNMIK Emergency Decree 1/1999 (June 28, 1999) and UNMIK Emergency Decree 2/1999 (June 28, 1999) creating the legal basis for JAC/PJA and appointing its members (three internationals and four locals—two Albanians, one Serb, and one Bosniak).

6. By 1993, 300 of 500 Albanian judges, prosecutors, and senior officials had been fired; the Serbian parliament named 168 new judges, of whom only twenty-five were Albanian, and of those, only sixteen took up their posts. Miranda Vickers, *Between Serb and Albanian: A History of Kosovo* (New York: Columbia University Press, 1998), p. 274.

7. Interview, Pec, September 26, 2000.

8. Article 197, FRY Code of Criminal Procedure.

9. "Withdraw Immunity Regulations, Ombudsman Warns Haekkerup," Radio B92 News, available online at http://www.b92.net/archive/e/index.phtml (accessed May 29, 2001).

10. UNMIK Regulation 1999/1, Articles 2 and 3 (July 25, 1999).

11. The regulation sowed some confusion. In case the 1989 law does not cover a given situation and a subsequent law does, the latter may be applied as long as it does not discriminate and does conform to international human rights law. Another provision allows for applying the "most favorable provision in the criminal laws which were in force in Kosovo between 22 March 1989 and the date of the present regulation." This complex menu of possible applicable laws invites problems and should have been avoided.

12. *Brahimi Panel Report on Peacekeeping,* available at www.un.org/peace/reports/peace_operations.

13. Kosovo has a supreme court, five district courts (Pristina, Mitrovica, Gnjilane, Prizren, and Pec), twenty-two municipal courts, one commercial court (Pristina), one high court of minor offenses (Pristina), twenty-two minor offenses courts, and thirteen offices of the public prosecutor.

14. "The Justice System of Kosovo: Basic Information," UNMIK, Administrative Department of Justice, September 11, 2000, p. 2.

15. Ibid.

16. This is the UCPMB, which first came to light in January 2000 and lay largely dormant until it killed four Serb police officers in November 2000. Violence escalated, and on December 17, insurgents fired on a joint U.S.-Russian KFOR patrol that had blown up a road used by the UCPMB to infiltrate weapons and men from Kosovo into the Presevo Valley. On the insurgency in Macedonia, see Carlotta Gall, "For Kosovars, Battle Moves to the Border of Macedonia," *New York Times,* February 25, 2001, p. A8, and Gall, "G.I.'s Join Macedonians in Fight Against

Albanian Rebels," *New York Times,* March 9, 2001, p. A4.

17. Interview, Pristina, September 22, 2000.

18. Ibid.

19. Interview, Pec, September 26, 2000.

20. Interview, Mitrovica, September 25, 2000.

21. Interview, Pristina, September 22, 2000.

22. Many of these officers were not trained or experienced prison guards; one senior UN official admitted that officers were routinely assigned to prison guard duty as "punishment" for poor performance. A CIVPOL officer who has worked in several Kosovo detention centers confirmed this.

23. Interview with senior UN official, Pristina, September 22, 2000.

24. Interview, Pristina, September 27, 2000.

25. KFOR Memorandum, Camp Bondsteel, October 18, 1999. U.S. army lawyers tracked numerous cases of ethnic bias they witnessed in hearings conducted by the mobile judicial unit that came three times a week to the detention facility at Camp Bondsteel. British army lawyers did the same regarding hearings held at the detention facility they maintained in Lipljan until early November 1999.

26. OSCE Mission in Kosovo, "The Treatment of Minorities by the Judicial System: Background Report," n. xxv.

27. KFOR memorandum, Camp Bondsteel, October 18, 1999.

28. Ibid.

29. OSCE, "The Treatment of Minorities by the Judicial System," n. xxvi.

30. Lawyers Committee for Human Rights, *A Fragile Peace: Laying the Foundations for Justice in Kosovo* (New York: LCHR, October 1999).

31. "European Lawyers Group Demands Release of Kosovo Murder Suspect," *Agence France-Presse,* August 6, 2000.

32. "Application: The Case of Afrim Zeqiri from the Village of Cernica in Gjilan," by Masar Morina, August 4, 2000.

33. I reviewed this videotape in January 2000.

34. Some of this summary is based on a thorough report on the case by the OSCE's Legal Systems Monitoring Section, "Justice on Trial: The Momcilovic Case," August 16, 2000.

35. Ibid., p. 7.

36. Ibid., p. 9.

37. Why it took almost a year for the U.S. military to provide this information remains a mystery.

38. The OSCE had prepared a plan that called for international judges in discussions in May/June 1999 during the formation of UNMIK. But this view was overruled by those who did not want to repeat the Bosnia approach, which had been criticized for its heavy international participation. This is an example of applying the wrong lessons from one operation to another, since Kosovo was very different from Bosnia in this regard.

39. An international judge later revealed that the French forces had arrested about twenty former members of the UCK for organizing the February 2000 riots in northern Mitrovica, including one who was wanted by Interpol. Yet French intelligence officers refused to share the results of their interviews with the judiciary and the men were all released. The judge maintains that UNMIK officials were responding to a threat by former leaders of the UCK to target KFOR troops unless the men were freed. R. Jeffrey Smith, "UN, NATO Criticized for Inaction on Violence," *Washington Post,* July 29, 2001, p. A1.

40. Interview, Pristina, September 22, 2000.

41. Interview, New York, February 26, 2001.

42. Quoted in R. Jeffrey Smith, "UN, NATO Criticized for Inaction on Violence," *Washington Post,* July 29, 2001 p. A1.

43. Nicholas Wood, "Amnesty and UN Staff Accuse Kosovo War Crimes Tribunal of Ethnic Bias," *Guardian,* June 23, 2001, available at http://www.guardian.co.uk/Archive/Article/0,4272,4206887,00.html

44. Ibid.

45. OSCE, *Six Month Report,* p. 48.

46. Ibid., p. 90.

47. OSCE, *Kosovo: A Review of the Criminal Justice System, 1 September 2000–28 February 2001* (Pristina: OSCE/LSMS, 2001).

7

Policing the Peace

Policing is a key element of the UN's efforts in Kosovo. UNMIK has focused on two initiatives to provide sound policing: deploying an international civilian police force (CIVPOL) and creating a new, local police force called the Kosovo Police Service (KPS).

CIVPOL

Deployment and Training

Modern UN peacekeeping operations now typically include a police component. Usually these international police are unarmed and monitor the performance of local police. They do not exercise "executive authority"— that is, the power to make arrests. The UN has seen, however, the need to step in and provide basic law and order in states that have basically disintegrated.

The UN had no choice in Kosovo but to provide security through armed police. As with the judiciary, all the police who had served under the Serb regime fled with the arrival of NATO forces. Very few Albanians had served in the police after 1989, and those who did were despised and distrusted. Unfortunately, many lessons identified from previous UN peacekeeping missions were not applied in Kosovo.

First and foremost, deployment of CIVPOL was agonizingly slow. Police officers, unlike their military colleagues, do not sit around station houses in their respective countries awaiting assignments or missions. They already have one: to provide security to the taxpayers who have hired them. Police are needed at home; most citizens and police force commanders believe they do not have enough police, so they are not happy to see dozens or even a few go off to the far corners of the earth. Police, with few exceptions, also do not have structures allowing rapid deployment as does the military; police are usually organized on a local basis and are not formed into battalions or divisions.

Although many experts called for countries to compile rosters of police who would be ready and able for quick deployment to overseas assignments, few countries had done so by June 1999. The overworked and badly understaffed CIVPOL unit in New York started a mad scramble to find police officers who could drop what they were doing and head off to a distant place. The first interim UN CIVPOL superintendent arrived in Kosovo a few days after NATO; he had to borrow a car and a radio and had no staff for several weeks.

CIVPOL's authorized strength in Kosovo is 4,718. This is the largest UN police force ever, dwarfing Haiti, Bosnia, Cambodia, and East Timor. As of September 2000, fifteen months after the start of the mission, this number had still not been reached. Only 3,222 were in theater; for most of the first twelve months CIVPOL had barely half its authorized strength.[1] The number reached 4,338 by the end of 2000 and 4,386 by August 2001. Special Police Units (SPU) were brought in from India and Pakistan in mid-2000. These units are highly trained in crowd control and are deployed as units so that problems of language, cohesion, and doctrine are minimized compared to the usual CIVPOL deployment, which involves police from many different countries assigned to the same station house.

SRSG Kouchner constantly bemoaned the shortage and pleaded with the Security Council and with member states, including his own country, France, to send police officers. While the shortage clearly hurt law enforcement efforts, the emphasis on quantity was misplaced. More important is the quality of the officers. Many CIVPOL interviewed stated that they would much rather have a smaller force of high-quality officers than the same number of quality officers dispersed in a larger, less competent force. The reasons: supervising and correcting the mistakes of the less able drains energy and morale; and the less qualified officers give the entire force a bad image.

Although the quality of CIVPOL in Kosovo is mixed, it is higher overall than in most previous missions. One important lesson implemented from earlier missions is the importance of predeployment screening. In Bosnia, for example, an entire group of CIVPOL officers had to be sent home once the UN Mission in Bosnia saw that they were not competent to perform their duties. This was embarrassing, expensive, and time consuming for the UN. In Kosovo, CIVPOL leadership assigned several members of its training unit to visit states that had offered to send police. The trainers administered several tests to the candidates: driving, English, and firearms. Those who passed were approved and those who did not never left their country. This helped improve the quality of the recruits, at least by eliminating the worst candidates. Some slipped through the net; one CIVPOL officer noted that "the English language skills, both reading and writing vary widely. A significant number of officers are functionally illiterate in the English language."[2] Some fifty police from Nepal and thirty-six from Bangladesh were placed on hold when they arrived, because the Nepalese arrived without handguns and most Bangladeshis were from administrative staff back home and had limited patrolling experience.[3]

An officer in the CIVPOL Training Unit notes that the two most frequent problems cited in disciplinary proceedings are sexual harassment and the use of force. Officers unaccustomed to working with women, either as peers or as subordinates to a woman commanding officer, have great difficulty in the multicultural environment common in CIVPOL missions; this is the case in Kosovo, where police come from fifty-three countries. CIVPOL leaders have increased training on awareness of sexual harassment in the workplace and have adopted a clear zero tolerance policy regarding sexual harassment. CIVPOL has adopted a code of conduct explicitly forbidding sexual harassment.

The use of force issue also reflects varying police practices, lack of training, and a failure to apply UN principles binding on all law enforcement officers. CIVPOL recognizes this problem, which is a vital one for any police force but especially for a force in a situation where the police routinely violated human rights with impunity. CIVPOL must show both the population and the new KPS impeccable behavior; any illegal use of force must be punished or else Kosovo risks never escaping from the violence that has characterized police-community relations for so long.

To its credit, CIVPOL has taken disciplinary action against police for using excessive force.[4] Some officers have been sent home to face proceedings. Others have been suspended or transferred. Training, especially on human rights and law enforcement, has improved. The human rights training given to newly arrived CIVPOL was limited and inadequate in the early months of the mission. The CIVPOL Training Unit has created a new five-hour module on human rights that reflects the reality of policing in Kosovo and reinforces core UN principles. For some officers this is their first exposure to human rights and policing, and CIVPOL missions can have the added benefit of spreading the human rights "gospel" back to the sending states as well as the receiving ones. Several CIVPOL officers promised to start human rights and community policing courses in their own police academies when they returned home.

One concrete example of CIVPOL officers' exposure to new issues is the question of domestic violence. This has also been a contentious question at the Kosovo police school and has led to changed attitudes and practices there. At the start, the CIVPOL Training Unit wisely included an expert on Kosovo culture to participate in the induction training received by all CIVPOL on their arrival. Unfortunately, CIVPOL invited the wrong expert. This person maintained that domestic violence is not only common but "accepted" in Albanian culture and that the international police should not intervene. To their credit, CIVPOL trainers found this position disturbing; they asked some other Kosovars, especially women, and found that the "expert's" opinion was anything but accurate or accepted. New trainers were found, and the handling of domestic abuse cases became a cornerstone of the CIVPOL training. CIVPOL even issued an operational bulletin, "Domestic Violence Enforcement Policy," which states that "UNMIK Police shall respond to and investigate all reported cases of domestic violence, regardless of who reports the crime. In addition, if probable cause exists that anyone involved in the household . . . has committed an act of domestic violence, they shall be arrested or detained in accordance with UNMIK Police policy."[5]

Some CIVPOL have not absorbed the seriousness of domestic violence. In one case, an off-duty CIVPOL officer found a woman bleeding on the street as a man beat her. The officer stopped a CIVPOL patrol car as it passed and asked them to help the woman. They refused, saying it was a private matter between a husband and his wife. The off-duty CIVPOL officer stopped the attack, arrested the man, and reported the other officers' behavior to the CIVPOL internal investigations unit. The officers were punished for their inaction.

Assessment of CIVPOL

Most CIVPOL are highly motivated and take their jobs seriously. I have seen police officers risk their lives in explosive situations; many work long hours in harsh physical surroundings. For example, an angry crowd of Serbs stopped a CIVPOL vehicle in northern Mitrovica on December 7, 2000, pulled out the CIVPOL officer and his female Serb interpreter, and beat both.[6] The Serbs were reacting to arrests and weapons searches made that morning by CIVPOL in connection with a murder case. On December 17, 2000, in the northern city of Leposavic, a Serb mob burned down the CIVPOL station and destroyed several police vehicles following the arrest of a Serb who tried to run a KFOR checkpoint. This Serb is a "bridge watcher," who made sure no Albanians crossed into northern Mitrovica; when he was arrested he reportedly tried to run over the Serb KPS officer who was there.[7] Others, both Albanian and Serb, have threatened to kill the arresting CIVPOL officer, saying they know where the officer lives. One German CIVPOL officer reported that his family back in Germany had received threatening phone calls because of his work in Kosovo. Nonetheless, many CIVPOL have donated their time and money to community projects. Others have not acted with such consummate professionalism and generosity.

Some Kosovars started derisively calling CIVPOL "Coca Cola cops," based on their red and white vehicles that uncannily resemble Coke cans. A seemingly large number of CIVPOL, especially in Pristina in the latter part of 1999 and early 2000, could be found in the city's many cafés and restaurants. Foot patrols were rare. "They stay in their vehicles and the local population says they are not approachable," according to one OSCE human rights officer. Some Kosovars and even the more dedicated CIVPOL believed that some international police were in Kosovo to make lots of money and to have an "adventure." Some officers were indeed reluctant to leave the station house or their vehicles.

Another possible reason for early CIVPOL passivity could have been a reluctance to be perceived as "neocolonialist," pushing reforms on the "uninformed locals." This is a common and understandable reaction across peacekeeping operations but should be anticipated and dealt with in training. CIVPOL initially was "too deferential and [did] not press hard enough for important reforms."[8] The right balance to strike in Kosovo between deferring and commanding needs continuous reassessment by CIVPOL leaders on the ground; some of this is a question of style of intervention: insisting on change without making people feel inferior or ignorant. This too requires providing good training and recruiting the right people. Kosovo in mid-1999 and throughout 2000, however, required a vigorous policing presence.

This passive, tentative approach eventually became the exception rather than the rule; CIVPOL leadership promoted more assertive, visible policing and increased contact with the community being served. Foot patrols increased and collaboration with KFOR also became common. The Royal Ulster Constabulary (RUC), with deep experience policing the challenging environment of Belfast, have been particularly effective in Kosovo. RUC officers frequently conduct foot patrols, search for weapons in cafés, and develop solid community contacts by engaging in a variety of non-police–related activities like building playgrounds, sponsoring neighborhood cleanups, and collecting toys for children. One Albanian human rights activist praised the RUC for their visible and proactive policing, saying that this is exactly the kind of tough and fair approach needed.[9] A police officer from Philadelphia noted that you had to be very firm, especially at the outset: "I have dealt with punks back home and the bad guys here are no different, especially the UCK. You have to show them right away who is the boss."

One major hurdle that CIVPOL and all law enforcement agencies, even the KPS, have tried to overcome is the reluctance of witnesses to give information. CIVPOL, prosecutors, and investigating judges have all had trouble getting statements from those who have either witnessed crimes or have information that would help solve crimes. In one heinous murder in October 1999, a newly arrived UN employee from Bulgaria was murdered on the busiest street in Pristina when he answered a query about the time in Serbian. He was immediately dragged away, surrounded by a crowd of at least 100 people, and killed. Yet CIVPOL and KFOR investigators could not get a single person to provide information on the killers. In another horrible case, a Serb university professor was beaten to death by a crowd in Pristina on November 28, 1999, Albanian Flag Day, when the car he was driving was stopped by a crowd. Someone recognized him and he was killed within minutes. His wife and mother-in-law were dragged out of the car and severely beaten. Some youths put firecrackers in the mouth of the mother-in-law and then lit and exploded them. She was rushed in a coma to a hospital in Nis, Serbia. KFOR and the police in this case also failed to elicit any information from the hundreds of people who witnessed this cruel murder and assault.

The reason people do not provide information is simple: they are terrified, and some are prejudiced. People fear that they will be killed if they give information to the police that would implicate powerful figures. "There is a strong code of silence here, based on terror, similar to what you see in parts of Italy regarding the Mafia," said one police expert who has worked in both places. This fear exists among Albanians and in the Serbian population, especially in northern Mitrovica where people close ranks and do not assist the police in criminal investigations.

Police report a gradual increase in the level of cooperation from the local Albanian community starting in the autumn of 2000. People grew more willing to provide information on crimes and appeared less fearful. Police suspect that many people are disgusted by the violence and want to see it stop. One leading Albanian said in September 2000, "I am really surprised by the level of violence. I never expected anything like this. We are ashamed, this shows we are uncivilized. Most people want peace, no more violence. People want jobs and economic development." Other Albanians interviewed shared this assessment. Some Albanians expressed similar revulsion after the bombing of a bus that killed eleven Serbs on February 16, 2001. The Geci family, for example, whose three brothers were in the UCK and who come from the Drenica Valley heartland, courageously condemned the bombing, saying it was "the most cowardly thing that had happened," and "we must find who did this."[10] Veton Surroi, alone among Albanian journalists, called the attack an act of terrorism.

One reason for increased cooperation with the police is that people see that CIVPOL is more assertive, visible, and effective. This can create a "virtuous cycle," where more assertive policing leads to more cooperation, which results in more effective policing and creates more incentives for the population to assist the police. Another reason is the steady decline in popularity of the UCK. The province-wide elections held on October 28, 2000, resulted in a crushing defeat of the UCK-based political parties by the moderate LDK led by Ibrahim Rugova. Rugova's party captured twenty-three of the twenty-six Albanian-majority municipalities and garnered almost 60 percent of the popular vote. This defeat was the most convincing indictment of the UCK's sponsorship of violence and extremism and has created hope that moderate Albanians will prevail in future elections.

CIVPOL and KFOR Cooperation

Visible, robust, and community-focused policing works best in peacekeeping operations, and both CIVPOL and KFOR soon saw that it was in their own best interest to collaborate and act more energetically. Adopting a bunker mentality was the surest way to failure. Each enhanced the other's "force protection," always a serious and natural concern, by adopting more proactive tactics.

Many who study peacekeeping emphasize the differences between the police and the military. While these differences do and should exist, they should not obscure the need for closer collaboration that will draw on the unique skills and training of each. The nature of the security threat in Kosovo requires close military and police coordination. I would argue that instead of constantly trying to demarcate policing from military action, or distinguishing how they are different, we should be trying to see where they overlap, merge, and can reinforce each other. This is true in Kosovo and could be a lesson for other postconflict situations. Joint military-police training and doctrine are needed.[11]

In Kosovo, the security threat on any given day ranges from rampant common crime; to mortars launched from hills; to new landmines being planted; to increasingly violent organized crime involving the drug trade, trafficking in women, and stolen cars and cigarettes; to planned provocations by Serb extremists in northern Mitrovica and insurgency operations by Albanian extremists along the borders with Serbia and Macedonia. And all may involve the same perpetrators or people closely linked. KFOR and CIVPOL must work together to control these threats. As one police officer from a small U.S. town said, "I don't see many rocket launchers and hand grenades in Bellevue, Washington, so I'm grateful KFOR are here." Joint KFOR-CIVPOL patrols are common and will be necessary for years.

Most of the violence in Kosovo stems from highly organized groups who have their own structures, hierarchies, command, and control. These include the ex-UCK, Serb extremists, and organized crime; in many cases there is an overlap between the former insurgents and organized crime on the Albanian side and between the former security forces and political hard-liners on the Serb side. KFOR intelligence services, working with CIVPOL special investigators and INTERPOL, have cracked several criminal enter-prises.

A good example of CIVPOL and KFOR collaboration occurred in November 2000, when after close observation a joint operation broke up a trafficking-in-women network and prostitution ring in the town of Fushe Kosov/Kosovo Polje. Seven men were arrested, including several believed to be former UCK members. Twelve women from Moldova were freed from what amounted to sexual slavery; after giving statements to the local judici-ary, they were offered the chance to go home.[12] Ironically, the trafficking and prostitution scheme required considerable collaboration between local Albanian and Serb pimps, which shows that interethnic cooperation exists. The successful raid followed the creation of a specialized CIVPOL unit focusing on trafficking in women and prostitution, which are major prob-lems in Kosovo.[13] Another series of joint operations rescued forty-five traf-ficked women in one week in June 2001, showing both the increased effec-tiveness of CIVPOL and the continuing problem of trafficking in women. CIVPOL and UNMIK need enhanced intelligence and more specialized units to combat organized crime and underground armed groups.

CIVPOL and KFOR have adopted special protection strategies for the ethnic minorities. Unannounced and random foot patrols and checkpoints keep the perpetrators of violence off-balance. Searching vehicles, especial-ly those without proper registration plates or papers, has yielded many weapons and helped prevent violence.[14] Setting up emergency hotlines and providing phones for minorities in their enclaves and using minority inter-preters to field these calls have improved both the reality and the percep-tion of security. Putting in speed bumps in the roads that go near or through the enclaves or go past the remaining Serb churches and monasteries has helped deter attacks. KFOR has also built bypass roads allowing Serbs to travel from one enclave to another without passing through heavily Albanian populated areas. Reinforced steel doors for minority-occupied apartments have also helped. And in a few cases, sentries have guarded the residences of some minorities in Pristina and Podujevo twenty-four hours a day, seven days a week.

British KFOR in particular have always responded positively to requests for innovative security measures. British soldiers escort Serb chil-dren to and from school every day in certain areas, and neither the children nor the soldiers complain. Russian and Spanish troops provide similar escorts to minority children in their respective areas of operation. In the greater Pristina area, especially near Slivovo, British KFOR launched Operation Trojan after consulting with the locals and coordinating with var-ious UNMIK agencies. The British arrange for water and power to be provided to this Serb enclave, and voluntary returns have increased. Equally important, the British are providing development assistance to neighboring Albanian villages so that they do not resent the help given to the Serbs. This novel and expansive approach to security has increased protection for all in this area.

Some KFOR contingents have generously shared their equipment and logistical heft with the more poorly equipped CIVPOL. For example, German KFOR in Prizren have assigned four MPs and crime scene equipment to the CIVPOL contingent there. Without this equipment many crimes would not have been properly investigated.

Collaboration between KFOR and UNMIK police is not, however, perfect. This is especially the case where powerful Kosovo Albanians are implicated in violence. Force protection is KFOR's overriding goal, and senior UNMIK officials often fear "alienating" Albanian leaders. British air force squadron leader Roy Brown, chief spokesman for the NATO-led peacekeeping force, freely admitted that KFOR "is willing to 'act against high-profile individuals' and frequently shares information with police. But it also must follow 'constraints imposed by the national security considerations of the thirty-nine nations that contribute to KFOR.'"[15]

Security Assessments

One annoying habit of both CIVPOL and KFOR, along with UNMIK, is to try to compare Kosovo's crime situation to that of other cities. It does no good to maintain, as did former U.S. secretary of state Albright, Lord Robertson of NATO, and others that the murder rate in Kosovo is lower than in Detroit, Berlin, Moscow, or wherever. This is irrelevant; ask a Serb or Roma if they feel safer today than they did in early 2000. Many incidents go unreported. As UNHCR and OSCE note in their Sixth Joint Report on Minorities in October 2000, low-level, constant harassment takes its toll, and one cannot say that any ethnic group in Kosovo has achieved a "lasting improvement in overall security."[16] Threatening phone calls, mysterious knocks on the door, nocturnal visits, and rocks through windows gnaw away at one's sense of security. The effect on minorities of long-term restricted freedom creates a siege mentality that is most pernicious.

Any decrease in murder stems largely from the enforced self-segregation most minorities have adopted to survive; they rarely leave their enclaves without military escort, and even this is not fail-safe. Just over one year after the rocket attack on a UNHCR bus near Banja, two buses filled with Serbs being escorted by KFOR were attacked in one week in February 2001. In the first, the bus driver was killed by a sniper near the Serb enclave of Strpce; the killer hoped that the bus would then crash in a nearby ravine killing many more, but fortunately this did not happen. In the second, 100 kilos of explosives destroyed a bus of Serbs returning from Serbia on February 16 to visit family graves the next day on the Orthodox day of the dead. This was a complex operation: the killers let two Swedish armored personnel carriers filled with the explosives go over the culvert and then detonated the device from 400 meters away at the moment the bus crossed. Body parts were thrown all over nearby fields, and identifying the dead, numbering eleven, was difficult.[17] Alert KFOR troops prevented a similar tragedy when they found and disarmed another explosive device placed in a culvert under a road close to a school in a mainly Ashkalia neighborhood near Lipljan on March 24, 2001.[18]

Based on their percentage of the population, a Kosovo Serb is ten times more likely to be killed than a Kosovo Albanian, and the murder rate for Albanians is already high.[19] This effort to show "progress" exemplified one of UNMIK's and KFOR's greatest flaws: spinning information to make it appear that the situation in Kosovo is "under control" when this is not the case. While achievements have occurred in some areas, it is counterproductive to overlook or downplay the real, persistent, and shocking level of violence in Kosovo. For too long, this is what UNMIK and KFOR did. What the Brahimi panel on peacekeeping recommended to the UN Secretariat holds equally true for UNMIK and other peacekeeping missions: don't tell the world or the Security Council what you think they want to hear; tell the truth, unvarnished, however unpleasant and ugly.

A mere glance at the daily police blotter shows that Kosovo is not like Berlin, London, or Barcelona when it comes to violence and crime. In just a ten-day period in October 2000, more than fifteen months after UNMIK and KFOR took control, here is a sampling:

October 15, Mitrovica North. A Turkish female reported that three Albanians came to her residence and threatened to bomb her flat because she lives with Serbs.

October 17, Shudrun Village, Vitina. Four Albanians reported that an Albanian male threw two grenades at them. While CIVPOL investigated, another Albanian male shot at them and the victims with an automatic rifle.

October 18, Stimlje. An unknown person threw a grenade at a Roma house injuring two females seriously.

October 21, Glogovac. A search operation resulted in the confiscation of two rifles, three grenades, one pistol, three AK-47 magazines, two flak jackets, one cocking lever, a mortar sight, periscope binoculars, a radio charger, and 107 types of ammunition.

October 22, Djakovica. A local leader of the LDK found an unexploded hand grenade in the rear garden of his home. Another LDK leader reported that an unknown person threw a grenade at his home.

October 25, Vitina. A Serbian home was damaged by a grenade attack and gunfire.

October 25, Urosevac. An inhabited Albanian residence was the target of a grenade attack. No one was injured.[20]

UNMIK, KFOR, and CIVPOL do a disservice to themselves by downplaying the seriousness of the violence in Kosovo, which they are combating with increasing vigor and creativity.

Confusion over the Applicable Law: Impact on Policing

The confusion over which law applied in Kosovo had practical consequences on CIVPOL's work. Officers literally did not know what criminal procedure law to apply, so many just applied what they knew from home. One CIVPOL officer noted, "We were like babies when we arrived. We knew nothing about the local law. We were lost. We each based what we did on the law from home. I was most concerned about saving face."[21] Another CIVPOL officer stated that some officers did not want to follow guidelines that are accepted in "modern countries" and felt they could do as they pleased; they operated in a vacuum most of the time.[22]

CIVPOL officers also had an up-close view of the deficiencies in Kosovo legal practice. In one case, two CIVPOL officers asked for guidance from UNMIK's Human Rights Office. An Albanian judge had instructed them to "beat the suspect if he doesn't give you information." The judge said this is how interrogations had always been conducted in Kosovo and it was the best and quickest way to obtain confessions. To their credit, the UN police refused to follow this order, but they still did not know what laws governed interrogations and how to respond to this judge and others who might make similar assertions.

UNMIK took too long to develop a training package on applicable Kosovo criminal law and procedure for UN police. Months after the applicable law question was settled in December 1999, there was still no adequate guidance. Finally, in September 2000, UNMIK's Administrative Department of Judicial Affairs prepared a short guide to applicable criminal procedure law for UN police. This thirty-page guide is used in two-day training sessions for CIVPOL, KFOR, and OSCE trainers.[23]

CIVPOL and the KPS

UN police play a key role in the KPS training. After nine weeks at the police school in Vucitrn, KPS cadets arrive for nineteen weeks of on-the-job training in all districts of Kosovo. CIVPOL officers act as "mentors" to the KPS; their job is to "explain, demonstrate, observe and critique."[24] The CIVPOL officer explains how to search a car or make an arrest, demonstrates the procedure, and then observes and critiques the KPS officer. This is an excellent way to extend and deepen the trainee's knowledge, and it literally buys time for the newly created police force to develop the skills and obtain the experience necessary until the KPS can take over policing.

A few problems have developed with the field training officer (FTO). First, some of the CIVPOL themselves are ill suited for mentoring newly trained, rookie police officers. Lacking facility in English or even in basic policing skills, some FTOs are poor role models or mentors. Some send exactly the wrong message on proper policing, especially those FTOs with limited knowledge of human rights or community policing principles. Those who are passive and exhibit little interest in preventing crime or forging strong ties with the community should not be FTOs. Some CIVPOL who are retired police officers back home have exactly the maturity, judgment, and experience essential for good mentoring.

Another problem is that as more KPS officers have graduated from the training school, the ratio of FTOs to KPS personnel has deteriorated. In the early days, there was a one-to-one relationship and the FTO could closely observe and critique the KPS officer. Real mentoring took place as did solid learning. By December 2000, however, it was not unusual to see one CIVPOL being trailed by six or seven KPS on foot patrol or a CIVPOL vehicle jammed with KPS, an interpreter, and the FTO. It is impossible, according to police experts, to do proper field training in these circumstances. CIVPOL faces a real numbers crunch, because they need all available officers to do frontline police work and can't spare many more for FTO mentoring. Yet the KPS also needs to produce officers quickly. One officer described a typical scenario: "There are not enough FTOs to go around. At this moment there are eight KPS officers standing at the HQ building entrance. They are there all day long and into the evening. There is nothing else for them to do."[25] According to this officer, most FTOs are serious and do their best under trying conditions.

CIVPOL leadership has created a corps of primary field training officers who assess the performance of FTOs to ensure quality control. These officers grade the performance of FTOs and recommend transfers for those unable to perform.

THE KOSOVO POLICE SERVICE

The Kosovo Police Service and its school in Vucitrn prove that multiethnicity is neither dead nor a pipe dream in Kosovo. It is one of two institutions in Kosovo, along with the fire department, in which Albanians, Serbs,

Roma, Turks, and Muslim Slavs work together and, in the school's case, live together. How the KPS has achieved this provides important lessons to Kosovars and internationals working there to construct a society based on the rule of law, tolerance, and respect.

KPS Training: The Police School

The OSCE, the UNMIK pillar in charge of institution building, has responsibility for creating a new police force for Kosovo. It undertook the task with gusto, taking over the site of the former police academy in Vucitrn, a city just south of Mitrovica that suffered much destruction at the hands of Serb forces. Rehabilitation work began in July 1999, and the school welcomed its first class in early September. The OSCE recruited police trainers from its member states to staff the school. Several had worked in Haiti helping to create the police training center there in 1995.

The UCK wanted its members to constitute the entire KPS; they argued that since the UCK had to disband as part of the cease-fire agreement, its fighters needed employment and deserved a spot in the new police force based on what they had sacrificed for Kosovo. The UN, with some KFOR backing, wisely resisted, realizing that this would be a mere subterfuge to keep the UCK intact and would also frighten both the remaining minorities and Albanian moderates. The opening of the school was delayed several times as negotiations continued. Finally, in early September, a deal was reached whereby the UCK was assured 50 percent of the places in the new KPS. While this percentage was still high, an important lesson was identified—but unfortunately not repeated often enough: UNMIK and KFOR would have to stand up to the UCK and other hard-liners and not be afraid to reject their demands. UNMIK and KFOR would have to push hard to ensure participation for moderate Albanians and minorities in all spheres.

From the very first class, the KPS has sought minorities. Recruiters visit minority enclaves and urge eligible candidates to apply. Applicants must be at least twenty-one, have at least a secondary school education, be a resident of Kosovo, be physically and mentally fit, and have no criminal history. The rigorous screening process consists of an oral interview, a written exam, a psychological test, a medical exam, a physical agility test, and a background investigation.[26] In a few cases, minority group members have complained that they did not receive applications in time; in one case, Albanian employees of UNMIK were suspected of dumping applications from minority members so that they were never considered. The OSCE took these accusations seriously and intensified its outreach efforts and security for minority applicants.

Some minority candidates, especially Serbs, face pressure from extremists not to join the KPS. The Serb hard-liners assert that Serbs should not "collaborate" with the UN or with Albanians, who only want to separate Kosovo from Serbia. Some minorities genuinely were afraid to travel and then live in Vucitrn, a town now almost completely Albanian. In several of the first few classes, only about one-half of the minorities who were accepted in the KPS actually showed up for the training. KFOR troops still provide armed escorts for Serbs to come for their training and then take them home at the end of the nine-week basic course. The school must conduct separate graduation ceremonies, since it would be too dangerous for the Serbs and other minorities and their families to come to Pristina for the main ceremony; likewise, it would be dangerous for Albanian KPS to enter Serb enclaves.

The goal for minority participation is 15 percent, corresponding to the percentage of minorities in prewar Kosovo.[27] The KPS classes of about 300 each have averaged 17 percent minorities. "When we get them we keep them," says school director Steve Bennett. Collegiality and cooperation are the dominant ethos of the school. Classes are not segregated by ethnicity. This means that presentations are given in English and then translated into Albanian and Serbian. The disadvantage is that the already short nine-week basic training is effectively further truncated by time taken for interpretation; the advantage is that an esprit de corps and cross-ethnic cooperation are cemented. The trainees live, eat, learn, and play together. The mission of serving all citizens as KPS officers, regardless of ethnicity, soon predominates.

Bennett cites several examples to illustrate the point. Several KPS cadets walked through Vucitrn to give a talk at a local school. Some townspeople yelled at them as they walked by, "Where are the Serbs?" The leader of the KPS group answered, "There are no Serbs, there are no Albanians, we are all KPS." He got no further guff from the crowd. In another case, several Albanian cadets saw that a few of their Serb classmates had moved into a room down the hall. The Albanians had several empty beds in their room and invited the Serbs to move in with them so that they could get to know each other better and study together. The Serbs accepted the invitation.

The cadets involved in the second example were women, and the KPS has made historic strides for Kosovo and the Balkans by making the recruitment of women a high priority. The KPS classes have averaged 18 percent women, an unheard of level for the police. Many of the best performers in each class have been women. At least one woman was the best "marksman" in the class. The presence of women has "lowered the testosterone level," according to several instructors. The TMK, the largely UCK entity charged with responding to civil disasters and emergencies, has even complained that the KPS has "too many women," which shows the prevailing mentality in the TMK. The women cadets are usually the first ones to reach out to the other ethnic groups.[28] The question of domestic violence, long explained away as "cultural" or swept under the rug, has received vigorous treatment in the KPS school; this would not have happened but for the presence of a critical mass of women. In early December 2000, a special three-day workshop on domestic violence was held in Pristina for KPS, KFOR, CIVPOL, the local judiciary, and NGOs. Once again, the women KPS officers were active and key participants in the conference, the first of its kind in Kosovo. The presence of women KPS officers has meant that women are more willing to report domestic abuse, and the female police officers have often taken the lead in combating prostitution and trafficking.

The average age of KPS officers is thirty-eight; the mean age is twenty-eight. Many of the former UCK members are older. About 25 percent of each class are former members of the pre-1989 police. These members also tend to be older but have extensive police experience from the days before Kosovo lost its autonomy and the police became primarily a Serb force. One disadvantage with this group is that they learned a different style of policing under a communist/socialist system. Human rights and community policing are foreign concepts, plus they must "unlearn" some lessons from their original training, such as blind obedience to commanders and unquestioning loyalty to the state. Some do have excellent leadership skills, management experience, and maturity, which are crucial in a force starting from scratch. The KPS has started specialized management training for KPS who have completed the basic training and the nineteen weeks of field training and who have shown leadership potential.

The basic course lasts nine weeks and is roughly 400 hours of instruction. The subjects covered include duties of a police officer, democratic policing, legal issues (taught by local lawyers), police skills, physical training, firearms, crime investigation, and self-defense. Human rights principles are incorporated in all subjects and are not taught as a separate topic.

By May 2001, the police school had trained 4,000 candidates in the basic course. In the same month, UNMIK announced that the KPS would have 6,000 officers, an increase of 1,500 from the original goal. UNMIK hoped to accelerate the process of local police taking over responsibility from CIVPOL. Nine hundred KPS managers and supervisors had undergone specialized training in addition to the basic course. Also, the KPS has specialized courses for correctional officers; by December 2000, 690 had completed a four-week basic training course. A multiethnic corps of local trainers will have been identified and trained, leading to a gradual handing over from international to local staff. Specialized courses in narcotics, criminal investigations, domestic violence, organized crime, forensics, and other subjects will be offered.

The KPS started conducting patrols on their own in the fall of 2000. While most are accompanied by CIVPOL mentors as part of field training or go on joint patrol with CIVPOL or KFOR, by December 2000, KPS could be seen on the beat or directing traffic in Pristina without international supervision. In Gnjilane, the KPS have made numerous drug arrests, thanks to having developed community contacts who provided crucial information.[29] KPS also visit the schools in the town to warn students about the dangers of drugs. This type of community policing is the cornerstone of KPS strategy.

Unfortunately, the KPS officers cannot yet patrol in ethnically mixed groups or work in areas where the population is of a different ethnicity. So Albanian KPS work in Albanian areas and Serbs work in the Serb enclaves. Other minorities work where their own safety will not be at risk.

Disciplinary Issues

Most Kosovars seem pleased with the KPS. All ethnic groups agree that they are doing a good job and that it is important that locals take on more of the police work.

As of September 2000, the KPS school reports that they had a loss rate of under 3 percent due to discipline issues. Three KPS had been terminated for criminal activity, five were suspended pending investigations, six were reprimanded for policy violations, and one was suspended for repeated policy violations. Five KPS had resigned. A CIVPOL officer recommends putting KPS internal investigations into the hands of the unit responsible for investigating alleged CIVPOL violations. This would remove double standards, give KPS officers the same rights and protections as international officers, and diminish the opportunities to intimidate investigators, who would be international.

Out on the beat, CIVPOL reports that KPS on the whole are highly motivated, disciplined, and eager to learn. CIVPOL believes that the training received at the KPS school is good but that the time is too short. The strong and understandable impetus to field a local police force quickly necessitates abbreviated basic training; a CIVPOL officer says that "because of the interpreting in the one-hour block courses, each class contains only twenty minutes of instruction. By extension, the nine-week course is realistically no longer than three or four weeks. This does not allow for an acceptable level of basic training."

Despite these numerous challenges, the KPS is clearly the crown jewel of the international community's initiatives in Kosovo. Unfortunately, the same cannot be said of the TMK.

NOTES

1. As of March 11, 2001, CIVPOL were deployed as follows: Pristina, 778; Prizren, 408; Pec, 302; Mitrovica, 521; Gnjilane, 368. The balance was assigned to headquarters, border police, training staff, Kosovo police/school, and special police units. UNMIK Daily Security Briefing, March 12, 2001.

2. Interview, Gnjilane, November 4, 2000.

3. Kevin Done and Robert Graham, "UN Doubts over Police for Kosovo," *Financial Times,* November 8, 1999.

4. Police have also been disciplined for involvement in prostitution. Two CIVPOL officers were sent home and two others reprimanded for transporting prostitutes in their vehicles in exchange for money from brothel owners and sex from the prostitutes. UNMIK, *News Update,* "Police Disciplined," August 13, 2001, available online at http://www.un.org/peace/kosovo/pages/kosovo.shtml.

5. UNMIK Police, Operational Bulletin No. 0034, September 13, 2000, par. 3.2.

6. "UN Police, Interpreter Beaten in Kosovo Weapons Raid," Reuters, December 7, 2000, (available at http://www.alertnet.org/newstory). The weapons search yielded eleven AK-47 assault rifles, nine antitank rockets, two packages of plastic explosives, a rifle, a pistol, and 1,500 rounds of ammunition—unfortunately a typical haul in Kosovo.

7. UNMIK press conference, December 18, 2000.

8. C. T. Call and W. Stanley, "A Sacrifice for Peace? Security for the General Public During Implementation of Peace Agreements (draft, November 1999), cited in David H. Bayley, "Democratizing the Police Abroad: What to Do and How to Do It (unpublished manuscript, October 2000).

9. Interview, Pristina, September 22, 2000.

10. Carlotta Gall, "Doing the Right Thing, in Kosovo's Heartland," *New York Times,* February 23, 2001.

11. In his memoirs, General Clark notes that the military should not do police work and that this is an important lesson from the intervention in Haiti. Yet he then describes an operation in Bosnia where the military, acting very much like police and working in close coordination with police, dealt effectively with an unruly crowd and a hostage situation. Gen. Wesley K. Clark, *Waging Modern War* (New York: Public Affairs, 2001), p. 98.

12. Nicholas Wood, "Kosovar Sex Slave Ring is Smashed," *The Guardian,* November 18, 2000. Several UCK members have engaged in criminal activity. Sabit Geci, a former UCK commander, was arrested the week before the Kosovo Polje raid after threatening to kill the owner of a strip bar; Geci was later involved in a fight in the Pristina jail where several inmates were injured. A crowd of demonstrators later prevented his trial—on charges of extortion, causing an explosion, and endangering lives—from starting on March 6, 2001.

13. In early 2001, UNMIK issued Regulation 4/2001, which criminalizes trafficking in persons; where the victim is younger than eighteen, convictions carry increased prison time. Persons who knowingly use the sexual services of a trafficked victim also face imprisonment.

14. After much urging, UNMIK finally issued a regulation in February 2001 sharply increasing the penalties for illegal weapons possession. See UNMIK Regulation 7/2001.

15. R. Jeffrey Smith, "UN, NATO Criticized for Inaction on Violence," *Washington Post,* July 29, 2001, p. A1.

16. UNHCR/OSCE, Sixth Joint Report on Minorities, October 2000.

17. Carlotta Gall, "Death Toll in the Kosovo Bomb Attack on Serbs Rises to 11," *New York Times,* February 18, 2001, p. A-4.

18. UNMIK Press Briefings, March 26, 2001, available at www.un.org/peace/Kosovo/briefing/pressbrief26mar01.html.

19. International Crisis Group, *Report Card on Kosovo,* available at www.crisisweb.org/projects/showreport.cfm?reportid=11, August 28, 2000, p. 16.

20. These excerpts were taken from the *New York Times,* "The War Is Over; Now, Violence Is the Daily Routine," October 29, 2000 (Week in Review section).

21. Interview, Pristina, September 27, 2000.

22. Interview, Prizren, December 25, 2000.

23. Interview with Sylvie Pantz, co-head of Administrative Department of Judicial Affairs, Pristina, September 24, 2000.

24. Interview with CIVPOL officer, Gnjilane, December 7, 2000.

25. Ibid.

26. The background check and the written exam cause most of the rejections. Interview with Steve Bennett, director, Kosovo Police School, Vucitrn, September 22, 2000.

27. The best estimate of the current minority population is 5–7 percent.

28. Interview with Steve Bennett, September 22, 2000.

29. Kosovo Press Briefings, at www.un/org/peace/kosovo/briefs/pressbriefs12march01.html.

8

The Kosovo Protection Corps

The Kosovo Protection Corps (Trupate E Mbrojtes te Kosoves, TMK) was created by virtue of UNMIK Regulation 8/1999. It is supposed to be the disarmed and demilitarized successor to the UCK. It is a civilian emergency response agency whose purposes are limited by law to providing disaster response services; performing search and rescue operations; providing a capacity for humanitarian assistance in isolated areas; assisting in demining activities; and contributing to rebuilding infrastructure and communities.

The same regulation expressly provides that the TMK "shall not have any role in law enforcement or the maintenance of law and order." Ten percent of its 5,000 membership slots are reserved for members of minority groups; however, only a few minorities had enrolled as of October 2000, and no Serbs had joined. The Bosniak TMK recruiter was severely beaten near Klina in October 2000 because of his efforts to enlist minorities.

It is an open secret that the TMK views itself as an army in waiting. According to UN officials, the idea to turn the UCK into some kind of benign civil emergency corps came from NATO. "NATO dropped this on us. They wanted to avoid any problems with the UCK but they passed this headache on to us. We had no chance to discuss this with NATO, it was imposed on us."[1] NATO believed that by creating the TMK they could somehow keep the old UCK officer corps under control and avoid any confrontations between NATO and UCK. The UCK leaders liked the idea because it was a way to conserve their force structure, identity, and influence. They would merely placate the UN and NATO on the surface, pretending not to be an army or public order force but in reality keeping many of the attributes of a military force, and await the day when this would become explicit and overt rather than covert.

The TMK's true intentions became apparent in the negotiations leading to its creation. There was much dispute over the name itself, which in

Albanian has a distinctly military and national defense connotation. Efforts to change the name failed as General Ceku and his team refused to yield. Another sticking point was the use of military ranks in the TMK, with the UCK leaders insisting on titles like general and colonel; UN/NATO negotiators proposed more civilian sounding ranks appropriate to a civilian organization involved in public service. The UCK negotiators also wanted military-style uniforms, including camouflage and high black boots. Once again, the UCK/TMK demands prevailed. The gap between NATO's intentions and the TMK's attitude was revealed in General Ceku's speech on September 21, 1999, marking the UCK's "farewell" parade through Pristina: "Today, we are ending the march of freedom but we are starting the march of the future for the independent Kosovo and its army."[2]

Since the TMK formally came into existence in January 2000, many in Kosovo, including Albanians, worry about its present and probable future activities, spurred by the TMK law enforcement activities that violate Regulation 8. Some Albanians and many KFOR and CIVPOL officers believe that a major security issue is whether the TMK will honor the regulation and, if not, whether members who violate the law will be punished. Some CIVPOL officers made their gloomy assessment clear by noting that TMK means "thugs mugging Kosovars."

UNMIK police interviewed were particularly vehement in expressing their frustration with the TMK, whose behavior includes arrests and detention, interrogations or "informative talks" (which often result in beatings of the detained), searches and seizures of property and persons, enforcement of illegal taxation schemes, evictions from property, and crowd control. This last activity became common after several demonstrations protesting the violence in Mitrovica in early February 2000. Unfortunately, in some cases, certain KFOR officials and UNMIK police invited TMK to play this role, which is essentially a "maintaining law and order" function prohibited by Regulation 8. The ongoing shortage of UNMIK police created a "security gap" quickly filled by TMK in some regions.

These reports of illegal activity and human rights abuses by TMK are not new. In the preliminary phase, starting in September 1999 when former UCK members began to apply for membership in the TMK, the Human Rights Unit of the SRSG's office, OSCE, and UNHCR investigated numerous and well-founded allegations of criminal activity by TMK applicants. In one typical case, a CIVPOL officer arrested three TMK applicants in late October 1999 for interrogating and beating an ethnic Albanian over a traffic accident; what was unusual about this case was that the victim was not intimidated and came to CIVPOL to give direct evidence against the accused. At TMK headquarters in Srbica/Skenderaj, an OSCE local staff member was taken and interrogated for one hour in November 1999. TMK in Prizren, either applicants or actual members, were calling people into its headquarters for the infamous "informative talks." CIVPOL noted at that time that the TMK was "getting out of hand" and had become a priority security issue for them. Incidents were so commonplace that UNMIK Police Daily Situation Reports had a separate section for the TMK.

Great confusion resulted from the decision to give TMK applicants an identity card, which many used to "authorize" their actions by asserting that they were already members. CIVPOL had trouble distinguishing between actual TMK members and applicants when they investigated crimes. Whether applicant or member, CIVPOL found that a large number of crimes and violent acts were perpetrated by people bearing these TMK cards and/or wearing military-style uniforms.

It was noted that half the slots in the Kosovo Police Service are reserved for former UCK members, leading many to fear that former UCK may unduly influence the KPS. The creation of the TMK as a successor to the UCK has intensified this fear. The TMK is composed almost entirely of former UCK. UNMIK police leadership hopes that the percentage of UCK in the future classes of the KPS will decrease, since former UCK already control the TMK. One concern is that the TMK will seek to dominate and influence the KPS; a second is that the two might turn on each other, creating the specter of battling public security forces established and funded by the UN and NATO. A CIVPOL officer states that the TMK is "attempting to influence and control the KPS . . . KPS officers have told us that they have been told by the TMK that the Internationals will not be here forever and they will be in charge."[3] One senior UN official noted, "We are very worried about the TMK, I think we have created a monster." The first KPS officer injured in the line of duty was shot by a TMK member after an argument.

Police experts maintain that newly formed police forces should not include people with records of human rights abuses or questionable behavior.[4] These people should be excluded because "not only may a new police force quickly become tainted by association with discredited personnel, but old behavior patterns may be passed on to new and impressionable recruits. It is especially dangerous to 'roll over' whole units into the new police."[5] While the TMK is not a police force, it has all the trappings of an army/police in waiting, and the dangers of "rolling over" the UCK into both the TMK and the KPS are real for each. Postconflict peacekeeping missions have frequently faced pressures to enlist demobilized combatants who allegedly possess management and supervisory skills that are in desperately short supply. Yet UNMIK and KFOR should have tried harder to leaven the management ranks of the TMK with people who were not UCK members and who have management and supervisory experience. The former UCK leaders in the TMK have brought "with them a cohesiveness that hampers change."[6]

In March 2000, journalists obtained a confidential internal report written by the SRSG's Human Rights Unit documenting human rights violations by TMK members. Instead of defending the report, some UNMIK officials sought to soften its impact by stating that the violations found in the report were often by TMK "candidates" and not actual sworn-in members. This sent the wrong signal to TMK leaders, who should have been told that illegal behavior by the TMK would not be tolerated. The TMK's record over the following months belied UNMIK's position when TMK members were arrested for a variety of abuses. Once again, it would have served Kosovo and the UN better to be firm and consistent at the beginning. But at least the leaked report pressured UNMIK and KFOR to watch carefully for any abusive or illegal behavior by the TMK. Sure enough, within one month, several senior TMK officers had been cashiered or disciplined and the corps faced increased, but not sufficient, oversight. Dozens of others were disciplined in the following months. In a June 5, 2000, report the Secretary-General noted that there had been thirty compliance violations a month.[7] The International Crisis Group, a well-known international NGO, reported that through mid-August 2000, UNMIK had amassed 177 incidents of noncompliance with internal standards.[8] Extortion and intimidation continued to be serious problems. One bar owner who served and employed Serbs received several threats from the TMK/KPC,[9] noting, "I've been stopped by KPC officers and asked to pay them protection money . . . I think I'm one of the few bar owners that doesn't pay any protection at all."[10] TMK have also threatened judges, especially when a TMK member has been arrested; in a few cases, releases quickly followed; judges would not reveal these threats out of fear and the knowledge that CIVPOL and KFOR could not protect them.

When the message gradually spread that KFOR was serious, TMK behavior improved, with reported compliance violations dropping to seven a month.[11] But the overall problem of organized crime and the TMK's links to violence remain. A senior U.S. military officer noted in September 2000 that a "thugocracy" prevails: "The mafia, the politicians and the so-called freedom fighters are all connected."[12] The TMK is "involved in unlawful police work, detentions and organized crime. . . . Illegal detentions are also common along with beatings," according to a CIVPOL officer.

KFOR and UNMIK's confidence in the TMK's commitment to demilitarization and a narrow public service role was badly shaken in June 2000 by the discovery of a huge weapons cache just a few kilometers from its headquarters near Srbica/Skenderaj in the Drenica Valley, the historic UCK heartland. The British commanding general in the area noted that there were enough weapons and ammunition to supply a full battalion. Informed sources in KFOR believe it is inconceivable that such a large stash of weapons could have been kept so close without senior TMK's knowledge or consent. In another unsettling incident, TMK commander Sami Lushtaku was involved in a brutal assault on a team doctor following a football match in Vucitrn; KFOR and CIVPOL did not arrest him immediately because of his position and connections with powerful political allies.[13] An OSCE official maintains that senior UNMIK officials ordered the police not to arrest Lushtaku on two separate occasions and he has never been prosecuted.

There was more bad news for the TMK in May 2001 when three people were arrested for the brutal murder of former UCK leader Ekrem Rexha, known as Commander Drini. Rexha was known for his probity and was helping UNMIK in an anticorruption campaign. All three suspects were members of the TMK.[14] Yet the U.S. government's reaction to the arrests was astonishing. The U.S. mission in Kosovo released a statement saying that "these arrests do not in any way reflect badly on the KPC [TMK] and its important role in Kosovo."[15] This could only be seen as a vote of confidence from the TMK's principal funder and most important ally, despite the nearly contemporaneous arrest in May of Hajrizi Isa, another senior TMK official, in connection with a grenade attack that injured seventeen people in a café in northern Mitrovica.

Another TMK member had been arrested a few weeks earlier as a suspect in the February 2001 bombing of a bus from Nis that killed eleven Serbs, including a two-year-old child. Florim Ejupi, a senior TMK official, however, escaped from detention in the U.S.-run Camp Bondsteel by using a wire-cutter allegedly passed to him in a pie delivered by relatives. KFOR intelligence reports concluded that other TMK members were part of a "terrorist cell" responsible for the bombing of the bus from Nis.

An independent Belgrade radio reported in May 2001 that SRSG Haekkerup would shrink the TMK from 5,000 to 3,000 members.[16] It was becoming impossible even for the TMK's apologists in UNMIK and KFOR to deny the mushrooming evidence of the corps' participation in premeditated violence against minorities and in organized crime (smuggling, trafficking in women, extortion, illegal seizure of apartments, prostitution). A confidential UN report prepared in late 2000 noted: "Many KPC members, in some cases high-ranking KPC officials, have ties with criminal organizations."[17]

The most devastating blow to the TMK came in June 2001 from its primary international backer. In contrast to defending the TMK just a month before, President Bush announced that the United States would freeze the assets of people it believed were supporting the ethnic Albanian fighters in Macedonia and in southern Serbia. Five names on the list were senior officers in the TMK. The five were banned from entering the United States and suspended by Haekkerup from the TMK.[18] Shortly before the announcement the chief of staff of the TMK had left to lead the Albanian rebels in

122 ━━━━━━━━━━━━━━━━━━━━━━━━━━━━━━━ WILLIAM G. O'NEILL

Macedonia. He was one of about thirty TMK members who "took leave" and are presumed by TMK Commander General Ceku to be fighting in Macedonia.[19] Also in June 2001, UNMIK tabled a regulation prohibiting "terrorism and exporting violence outside the territory." This was in response to the central role played by the TMK and former UCK in the conflicts in southern Serbia and Macedonia. One UN official in Pristina noted, "people are saying that finally the farce of the TMK is over."[20]

UNMIK and KFOR should have overseen more intensely the daily operations of the TMK. Members of the Joint Task Force on Minorities regularly conveyed information and concern about TMK violations of Regulation 8 and its members' violent and criminal activities to KFOR representatives, but KFOR chose to downplay the gravity of the problem at the outset. Just as the new KPS is a creation of the international community, so is the TMK. The KPS cannot operate without CIVPOL and OSCE supervision and control. The same should be true for the TMK. KFOR should have inserted teams in every TMK regional headquarters to monitor and mentor and provide ongoing, intense oversight with the power to overrule TMK decisions and to recommend disciplinary action in cases of noncompliance. The leeway and independence of action granted to the TMK was a mistake that is harder to correct as time passes. The TMK was treated as an independent actor in a way that the KPS never was. The difference in results is clear: the KPS's performance of its mandate and the trust it inspires among Kosovo's population, including all ethnic groups, is vastly superior to the record and popular assessment of the TMK.

KFOR and UNMIK should not coddle the TMK; rather they should observe the TMK's work closely, give them adequate resources to do the civil relief work they are supposed to do, and deal swiftly and fairly with any crimes, human rights abuses, or violations of the TMK's mandate.

NOTES

1. Interview with UN official, New York, February 23, 2001.
2. Laura Rozen, "KLA Demilitarization Deal Despite Last Minute Wrangles," September 21, 1999, at www.transnational.org/features/demilitarisationdeal.html.
3. Interview, Prizren, December 25, 2000.
4. UNMIK and KFOR tried to screen all applicants to the TMK; the attempt was in good faith, but inevitably some very bad candidates sneaked through. For example, Xhavit Elshani, a former UCK and now TMK member, was arrested on September 25 for the murder of two people in Prizren prison on June 11 and 17, 1999. KFOR Multinational Specialized Unit Regiment HQ, Pristina, press release (undated and on file with the author). In Klina, on November 29, 2000, UNMIK arrested a TMK member who was suspected of intimidating and coercing locals; illegal weapons were also found. UNMIK/KFOR Press Briefing, November 29,

2000, available at www.un.org/peace/kosovo/briefing/pressbrief29nov00. TMK members often are involved in violence, sometimes as the target. See "KPC Commander Skender Gashi Found Dead" (Gashi's body was found in Suva Reka with both hands cut off, according to a report in the local press), UN DPI press summary, September 27, 2000, available at http://intranet/DPI/html/mon/lmm210900.html.

5. David H. Bayley, "Democratizing the Police Abroad: What to Do and How to Do It," (October 2000), pp. 56–57.

6. Ibid., p. 57.

7. Report of the Secretary-General on the United Nations Interim Administration Mission in Kosovo, "Excerpt on the KPC," June 5, 2000.

8. International Crisis Group, Report Card on Kosovo, available at www.crisisweb.org/projects/howreport.cfm?reportid=11, August 28, 2000, p. 12.

9. The English acronym for the TMK is KPC, which stands for Kosovo Protection Corps, not to be confused with the KPS (Kosovo Police Service).

10. Nicholas Wood, "Kosovo Gripped by Racketeers," BBC News, April 2, 2000, available at http://news.bbc.co.uk/hi/english/world/europe/newsid_699000/699175.stm.

11. Problems continued, however. For example, on October 21, 2000, Bardel Mahmuti, a TMK officer, was arrested when his vehicle was stopped at a British KFOR checkpoint. He and his bodyguard were carrying weapons for which they had no valid permit. UNMIK-KFOR Press Briefing, October 23, 2000, available at http://www.un.org/peace/kosovo/briefing/pressbrief23oct.html. On September 24, another KPC officer was stopped and found to be carrying an illegal weapon. KFOR daily press release, #09-27, September 24, 2000.

12. Roberto Suro, "In Kosovo, an Uncertain Mission," Washington Post, September 20, 2000, p. A1.

13. Lushtaku was one of the earliest leaders of the UCK, training with Jashari in Albania in 1990. See Tim Judah, Kosovo: War and Revenge (New Haven: Yale University Press, 2000), p. 111.

14. "Arrests Over Kosovo Murder," BBC News, May 9, 2001 available online at http://www.bbc.co.uk/hi/english/world/europe/newsid_132000/1321515.stm.

15. Quoted in R. Jeffrey Smith, "UN, NATO Criticized for Inaction on Violence," Washington Post, July 29, 2001, p. A1.

16. Radio B92 News, May 29, 2001, available online at http://www.b92.net/archive/e/index.phtml.

17. R. Jeffrey Smith, "UN, NATO Criticized for Inaction on Violence," Washington Post, July 29, 2001, p. A1.

18. Chris Stephen, "UN Suspends Five Officials Accused of Helping Rebels," Irish Times, July 7, 2001, p. 13.

19. Carlotta Gall, "U.S. Attempts to Quiet Fighting in Macedonia May Backfire," New York Times, Aug. 6, 2001, p. A4.

20. Ibid.

9

Prisons and the Penal System

The third leg of the judicial triad after the justice system and law enforcement is the prison system. As were the first two legs, the penal system was left in shambles by the departing Serb regime. All corrections officials, prison guards, and administrators left, and the main penitentiary in Dubrava, outside Istok, had suffered heavy damage from both the Serbs and NATO bombing. Once again, UNMIK had to scramble quickly with few resources to respond to an urgent need.

During the first few months following the air campaign, KFOR assumed complete responsibility for detention. Several hundred people arrested by KFOR were held at Camp Bondsteel by U.S. troops, in Lipljan by British troops, and in Pec, Prizren, and Mitrovica by various KFOR contingents. UNMIK police held detainees in the police jail in Pristina. Conditions in all were spartan but acceptable. The ICRC had regular access to all detention centers as did OSCE human rights field officers. Serb and Albanian detainees had to be kept apart.

On November 30, 1999, UNMIK Civil Administration took over responsibility for the prison in Prizren, the first one to shift from KFOR to civilian control. The Kosovo Correctional Service (KCS), part of the Interim Administrative Department of Judicial Affairs, also began operating that day and ultimately will run all penal institutions. Personnel recruitment faced the usual difficulties of low salaries and a shortage of qualified candidates. Eventually, about 120 Kosovars received specialized training at the Kosovo police school by the end of 1999, and one year later, about 600 more had been trained and were employed by the KCS.

The detention facilities are in Prizren (KCS), Mitrovica (CIVPOL), Pristina (CIVPOL), Camp Bondsteel (KFOR), Gnjilane (CIVPOL), Pec (KCS), and Lipljan (KCS). The major problem thus far has been prison escapes, especially from Mitrovica. The prison there is in the northern, Serbian part of town; this prison and Camp Bondsteel are where Serb detainees are held. In late August 2000, fourteen Serb detainees escaped, the second large escape within months. Many of these fourteen had been indicted for war crimes. Their escape rocked UNMIK and caused deep concern among Albanians about the seriousness of the UN's effort to mount an effective judiciary. Serbs in the Mitrovica jail also went on several hunger strikes to protest their lengthy pre-indictment detention and what they perceived as bias in the judiciary.

The Dubrava prison has undergone substantial rebuilding and will be Kosovo's major prison for convicted criminals. Its ultimate capacity will be 520 prisoners. Lipljan's detention facility, also undergoing rehabilitation, will be used for women and juvenile offenders. Its capacity will be forty-six persons and it will also handle any overflow from other centers. A major concern is the lack of a facility for prisoners requiring mental health care. The current facility at Stimlje is something out of the Middle Ages, with the physically handicapped and normal healthy children mixed in with the mentally ill. People wander the grounds unsupervised and ill clothed. Despite heroic efforts by a team of nurses and mental health specialists from the Norwegian Red Cross, few programs are provided to the Stimlje facility population and no treatment is available. But as one Red Cross worker noted, it is the only place in Kosovo where Albanians are caring for Serbs and Roma.

Kosovo's high rate of violent crime means that it will need all the possible allotted prison space for the foreseeable future. With 435 murders alone counted in the last six months of 1999, and 1,306 incidents of arson, the courts, once they are fully functioning, will be generating a large number of people sentenced to prison. In addition, there is no current working system of bail, so most people arrested are kept in pretrial detention, further burdening the penal system. The KCS has called for urgent discussions to develop probation and parole systems as alternatives to incarceration. This modern approach is largely unknown in Kosovo and will require research, training, and funding. Noncustodial alternatives for juveniles will be especially important to curb further violence and try to end the cycle of revenge and hatred.

As with every other initiative in Kosovo, the effort to create a modern and humane penal system depends on enhancing overall security and resolving the question of Kosovo's future political status. The leaders of the KCS summarized the challenges of everyone working in Kosovo:

> The overall environment in Kosovo is characterized by rapid and sometimes bewildering change, high levels of uncertainty towards the future and a need for continuing international security and support in order to allow the reconstruction process to continue. Funding and expert support will be needed from the international community in order to build a sustainable correctional system.[1]

NOTE

1. Kosovo Correction Service, "Strategic Plan 2000–2001," (May 15, 2000), p. 4.

10

Preventing Future
Human Rights Abuses

HUMAN RIGHTS PROMOTION AND EDUCATION

UNMIK regrettably had no coherent plan for human rights education or promotion initiatives. Yet everyone, including most Kosovars, knew that to prevent further abuses and to instill basic concepts—for example, the presumption of innocence, individual and not collective guilt, nondiscrimination and tolerance—an intense and well-coordinated program was crucial.

When UNMIK tried to engage in human rights promotion, many Kosovars complained that the international community did not consult them adequately beforehand. This was a valid complaint. The local NGO community in Kosovo is vibrant and has had a long experience in developing and implementing projects. The ten years of Serb rule forced them underground so that the Albanians learned how to fend for themselves. Serbs also had various groups, some with an explicit focus on human rights. Roma, Muslim Slavs, and Turks also have organized into various groups. In the Serb and Albanian communities, some groups were more political than others, and a few were purely fronts for others. But OSCE workers and others with experience in Kosovo knew the people who were genuine human rights advocates. There is a talented group of locals with whom UNMIK should have been working from the beginning on human rights education and promotion.

Some of these local rights experts criticized UNMIK's failure to grasp a central human rights issue: people in Kosovo see human rights primarily as collective rights, with the rights of a group predominating over individual rights. This results from recent political struggles emphasizing group status. "In the former Yugoslavia, if you were labeled a minority you were screwed," said one Albanian working for an international agency.[1] This explains why for many, political autonomy trumps individual rights; self-governance in monoethnic units seems "safer" than enjoying minority

Albanian children in Orahovac.

rights in a multiethnic unit.[2] It is precisely this analysis that enlightened Kosovars seek to reverse with help from UNMIK and the OSCE.

INTERNATIONAL HUMAN RIGHTS CONFERENCE

One successful initiative was the International Conference on Human Rights held in Pristina on December 10–11, 1999. The first international conference on human rights ever held in Kosovo, it was timed to coincide with International Human Rights Day. The OSCE took the lead role in planning, funding, and organizing the conference, which was an enormous undertaking in a Kosovo still lacking in electricity, reliable phones, and passable roads.

The OSCE early on consulted closely with leading Kosovo human rights figures to determine which issues should be featured at the conference and whom to invite, locally and internationally. The Kosovo human rights community was integral to the planning and ultimate success of the conference. OSCE field officers canvassed their local human rights counterparts throughout the territory to get their views and to ensure that people from the regions could attend the conference in Pristina. This was especially challenging for areas like northern Mitrovica and the Kamenica area of southeastern Kosovo, where the Serbs and Roma live in enclaves.

KFOR and CIVPOL contributed greatly to the ultimate success of the conference by providing extra security both in Pristina and to those traveling from the regions. Serbs, Roma, Turks, and Muslim Slav representatives all were able to attend because many came in KFOR armored personnel carriers to and from Pristina. For the minorities, it was the first time most had been back in Pristina since the end of the NATO air campaign. They were able to see old friends from all ethnic groups. One Serb lawyer from northern Mitrovica said he saw former Albanian colleagues of the Mitrovica bar and was able to discuss legal issues with them, including the war crimes indictments. He had not been able to contact them since the end of the war because they were now in southern Mitrovica; he hoped that he would be able to maintain communications.

Several leading international human rights experts came to the conference, including Bertie Ramcharan, deputy high commissioner for human rights; Thomas Hammarberg, former secretary-general of Amnesty International and a leading expert on the rights of the child; and Sir Nigel Rodley, UN special rapporteur on torture. These international experts participated in lively panel discussions and workshops with their Kosovo colleagues over the two days. Topics that the conference working group had identified for treatment were missing persons, property rights, children's rights, postconflict justice, the building of a new police force, torture, women's rights, and economic, social, and cultural rights.

During breaks, different cultural groups performed in a large reception area: an Albanian choir, Turkish teenage folk dancers, and a marvelous group of Roma children who danced and sang. The artwork by local painters and sculptors on exhibit showed the rich cultural diversity of Kosovo. For once, there was a neutral space where all ethnic groups in Kosovo could gather, if only for two days, to eat, drink, and talk in their own languages.

The conference was a success. Over 400 people attended. Some had difficult things to say and to hear, but it was all done in an atmosphere of mutual respect. The real suffering of the Albanians under Serb rule was eloquently expressed, pleas for finding the missing of all ethnicities rang through the hall, and everyone agreed on the need to focus much more attention on Kosovo's overwhelmingly youthful population. An excellent report of the conference, including all presentations and summaries of the workshops, was published by the OSCE, and its most important findings were translated into Albanian and Serbian.[3]

PUBLIC AWARENESS CAMPAIGN

Everyone connected with the conference realized that a more sustained effort to promote human rights was needed; the conference was a good launching point but was not sufficient to change minds and attitudes. This would take much longer.

With help from the Council of Europe, the OSCE brought a consultant to Kosovo who met with dozens of local NGOs, key individuals in the struggle for human rights, and members of UNMIK to get their views on how best to structure a public awareness campaign on human rights. Working with a local artist, the consultant came up with several ideas for posters, jingles, and other simple tools to begin to get people thinking about rights. The approach would encourage discussion, debate, and reflection and would not preach or repeat received wisdom.

The campaign formulated the phrase "The 10th of December is coming" as its keynote message. Soon posters in all the relevant languages (Albanian, Serbian, Roma, Turkish, and English) appeared all over Kosovo with this message. The point was to get people talking about rights and to create interest. One grocery shop owner in Kosovo Polje proudly had posters in both Albanian and Serbian in his shop to show that all were welcome and that he did not discriminate. In other places, however, posters in one language only were displayed, a sharp reminder of the work lying ahead.

OSCE NATIONAL HUMAN RIGHTS OFFICERS

One of the OSCE's most important capacity-building projects is the recruitment and training of national human rights officers. Numbering ten, these human rights professionals come from Albanian, Serb, and Slavic Muslim ethnicities. After receiving training on human rights law and on how to conduct an investigation, interview witnesses, and write a report, these officers go out in the field and work alongside their international colleagues. Each OSCE Human Rights Regional Office has two nationals. They do much more than mere interpreting, and as they gain experience they receive more and more responsibility. As with CIVPOL and the KPS, the international human rights monitors mentor the national officers, giving them on-the-job training and assessments of their work. This experience creates a corps of highly trained and skilled local human rights experts who will stay in Kosovo long after the internationals depart. This is "sustainable" human rights capacity building at its best.

HUMAN RIGHTS EDUCATION IN THE SCHOOLS

UNMIK's Pillar Two, Civil Administration, has a Department of Education responsible for developing curriculum and training teachers for all of

Kosovo's schools. As a result of the Joint Administrative Structure created in December 1999, the Department of Education is headed jointly by an international and a Kosovar.

The department was slow in developing a curriculum on human rights, despite the great and expressed need. As of January 2001, human rights remained absent from the curriculum. Into this vacuum OSCE human rights field officers and sometimes representatives of UNCHR and UNICEF have stepped to provide materials and instruction on human rights. Field officers have spoken to grade school and high school children about rights, using such teaching tools as role playing, games, and case studies. Several lawyers at OSCE headquarters have given classes on human rights and humanitarian law at the law faculty in Pristina. But these ad hoc activities cannot replace a planned human rights education program. Teacher training was overlooked for months.

KFOR soldiers have initiated peace and tolerance classes in some schools. The Spanish contingent in western Kosovo has taught such classes in Spanish to elementary school children who learn about peace and Spanish at the same time. This is also a novel way for KFOR to increase its ability to communicate with the local population. In one revealing lesson, children responded that flowers to them mean death, probably because almost the only time kids see flowers these days is at funerals. CIVPOL and KPS officers have also started to visit schools regularly to discuss traffic safety, drug and alcohol abuse, and the need to be wary of strangers; this last point is crucial given the number of abductions of young girls.

The office of the UNHCHR has extensive expertise and experience in human rights education at all levels. It has prepared teaching materials screened and approved by education experts. UNHCHR should take a much more active role in this crucial area; OSCE itself admits that it has limited experience in human rights education and the officials at UNMIK's Pillar Two need expert advice. This issue is too important for further delay; two school years have already gone by, and Kosovo's children need to be exposed to a human rights culture immediately, especially since some are committing human rights abuses already. This is one of the most disheartening aspects of the situation in Kosovo. Kids as young as eight have thrown rocks at Serb and Roma houses. Children slightly older have set fires to houses of minorities, especially Roma/Ashkalia quarters in Ferizaj/Urosevac. Others, often teenagers, have beaten elderly Serbs in Pristina, the Zupa Valley, and Prizren.

One CIVPOL officer noted that adults were intentionally using children to commit crimes, knowing they will be released immediately because neither KFOR nor CIVPOL has any facility for holding juvenile offenders and there is no juvenile justice system. This cynical use of children confers a form of impunity on the parents while contaminating the children with hatred and inuring them to violence. Unless addressed, this behavior will ensure that another generation in Kosovo will perpetuate hatred and violence.

UNICEF, as the lead agency in this area, created an emergency task force on juvenile justice, modeled on the successful Joint Task Force on Minorities. Convening all the major actors every other week, UNICEF spearheaded the drafting of an emergency regulation dealing with juvenile justice. Also, KFOR threatened to arrest the parents of a child apprehended for violent acts if the child was caught repeating the misbehavior. This has deterred some violence but is not the ideal solution.

FREEDOM OF EXPRESSION AND THE MEDIA

As with all other aspects of life, the Serbs dominated the media during the ten years of stripped autonomy. Albanians had limited access to all forms of media and the press was tightly controlled. With the arrival of NATO and UNMIK, Albanians quickly reclaimed posts at venerable newspapers and radio stations that finally could resume reporting.

Kiosks in Kosovo cities soon displayed numerous Albanian language newspapers that reflected various political party platforms. *Koha Ditore* was widely viewed as the most independent and reliable paper. Serb papers appeared only in the Serb enclaves and were brought in from Serbia proper. A Turkish weekly broadsheet appeared in Prizren and sometimes in Pristina.

Most of the press most of the time has acted responsibly. While many journalists need and welcome training to enhance their professionalism, a few have engaged in inciting violence and ethnic hatred. This poses a dilemma for UNMIK and KFOR, who understandably want to encourage freedom of expression. But freedom of expression has limits under international law, and identifying the exact location of these limits is not simple.

An early case arose in the fall of 1999 in Gnjilane. A radio station there broadcast the names and addresses of several Serbian families still living in the town. KFOR correctly saw this as a direct and immediate incitement to violence because at the time Serb houses were targets of grenades, mortars, and arson. KFOR warned the radio station to stop these broadcasts; when it did not, KFOR temporarily shut down the station. An important lesson had been learned from Rwanda, where a radio station run by Hutu extremists broadcast hate speech directed at Tutsis and urged all Hutus to "do their work," which everyone knew meant kill Tutsis. The UN force commander, General Dallaire, had asked UN headquarters in New York for authorization to stop these broadcasts but was refused. Radio Milles Collines played a key role in the genocide.

The next test for press freedom came in the summer of 2000; the Albanian language daily *Dita* published the name, address, and picture of a Serb named Petar Topoljski, whom the paper accused of having committed crimes against Albanians. Topoljski worked as a translator for UNMIK. He was murdered shortly after the article appeared. SRSG Kouchner ordered the paper closed for eight days. On reopening, *Dita* published the same article again, and this time UNMIK sought to impose a code of conduct on journalists. In a regulation issued on June 17, UNMIK created a temporary news media commission that has the power to impose fines, seize equipment or materials, and shut down the paper or broadcast medium. A board can hear appeals.

Kouchner's regulation launched a spirited debate about press freedom and responsibility among Kosovo journalists. Many opposed his efforts to dictate a code of conduct and thought that shutting down the press smacked of old-fashioned communism and could set a terrible precedent for Kosovo.[4] Some in UNMIK applauded the SRSG's strong stance and wished he had acted similarly on other issues earlier to show that ethnic intolerance would not be tolerated.

The SRSG had a good dose of international law on his side: Article 20 of the International Covenant on Civil and Political Rights prohibits "any advocacy of national, racial or religious hatred that constitutes incitement to discrimination, hostility or violence." Article 19 of the same covenant allows for certain restrictions on expression that are established by law and are necessary: "(a) For respect of the rights and reputations of others; (b) For the protection of national security or of public order . . . or of public health or morals." While closing down press outlets should be a last resort, when lives are at stake certain measures are required and allowed. The best result would be that these incidents have increased journalists' awareness of both their rights and responsibilities, thus improving the quality of reporting.

NOTES

1. Interview, Pristina, September 21, 2000.
2. Former president Gligorev of Macedonia summed this up perfectly: "Why should I be a minority in your state when you can be one in mine?" quoted in Susan Woodward, *Balkan Tragedy* (Washington, D.C.: Brookings Institution 1995), p. 108.
3. OSCE Mission in Kosovo, *Kosovo International Human Rights Conference, 10–11 December 1999, Conference Documents and Report.*
4. Steven Erlanger, "Death of Serb Named in Newspaper Sets Off a Battle Over News Media Restrictions in Kosovo," *New York Times,* July 13, 2000.

11

Conclusion

This study has tried to show that UNMIK and NATO have made avoidable mistakes by failing to apply several lessons identified in previous peacekeeping operations. The famous quote from the Irish writer Samuel Beckett comes to mind: "Try again, fail again, fail better."

A lesson emerging from Kosovo is that the UN, NATO, or regional bodies must marginalize the extremists, not the moderates. This underscores the importance of having topflight political advice and intelligence. The Department of Political Affairs should continue to have a central role in providing political advice to an SRSG; DPA should not be left behind when the UN Department of Peacekeeping Operations (DPKO) takes over an operation. The loudest and the most visible local leaders are often not the most popular or representative, as the October 2000 local elections in Kosovo demonstrated. The same holds true for the Serbian political class. Working with quality local political leaders is essential to building peace. In East Timor, the UN has forged a partnership with leaders of the highest caliber; in Kosovo it has not.

The UN and NATO must plan ahead so that they come in on day one with a comprehensive and coherent law enforcement capacity. The military must be ready to dedicate some of its personnel to police work, including arrests, detentions, and crowd control. This is unavoidable given current DPKO constraints on rapid deployment of CIVPOL. There will never be enough competent CIVPOL in theater soon enough. Also, one should not exaggerate the differences between "police work" and military tasks in environments like Kosovo, East Timor, and Bosnia, where the security threats often embody elements of each. The violence in most current conflicts does not respect the niceties of cleanly separating police and military tasks. Therefore, the tempo of joint international military and police training (ideally predeployment) should increase, as should doctrine on joint military and police operations in theater.

Many who have worked in peacekeeping operations bemoan the failure of the various participants to coordinate activities. Some maintain that it wholly depends on having the right people. However, Kosovo shows that coordination works best when there is a specific and concrete issue around which different actors coalesce. The Joint Task Force on Minorities is an excellent example of how coordination should work in a complex peacekeeping operation.

With a complete disintegration of the state (Kosovo, East Timor, Haiti, and Sierra Leone), international military and police must act robustly within limits set by international human rights and humanitarian law and make clear that all other armed elements must do likewise or else they will be arrested and prosecuted. There should be no tolerance for intolerance or revenge. Extremists and "spoilers" cannot be allowed to control the agenda.

The UN, NATO, or other military organization must not be afraid to declare martial law and must be prepared to suspend some human rights as necessary and allowed by international human rights law. If certain rights must be abrogated, the UN administration should follow established procedures, declare what it is doing and why, and lift such suspensions as soon as possible. Kosovo in the summer and fall of 1999 and parts of Kosovo today require derogations as allowed by the International Covenant on Civil and Political Rights. This can paradoxically lead to more widespread protection and observance of human rights. Many innocent people's rights were and are violated in Kosovo because of a failure to take concerted action against the perpetrators of violence.

A lesson identified in Haiti, Rwanda, Bosnia, and Cambodia but not applied in Kosovo is that it is never too early to restore the justice system. Where ethnic polarization precludes fairness and endangers those trying to be impartial, international jurists should take over key posts in cases where local jurists would not be able to act independently and in safety. Just as policing is not left only to the locals, neither should the prosecuting and judging. Failing to recognize this need can undermine the entire judicial reform effort.

The Kosovo experience confirms the Brahimi panel's finding that the UN should have modern, generic criminal law and criminal procedure codes ready and declare them to be the provisional applicable law in situations like Kosovo, where there is no clear-cut, acceptable alternative. The UN should avoid both a legal vacuum or a wasteful dispute over which local law prevails.

Responsibility for judicial reform should be centralized, with one line of command and control. Spreading responsibility among different parts of UNMIK has created turf battles, duplication of effort, and missed opportunities; it has also created confusion among Kosovar partners.

The UN should emphasize "quick-impact" projects in all spheres. It is crucial to get the trash picked up, traffic lights working, and public transport running. This shows the population both that things will be different and that someone is in charge. This will help prevent illegal parallel structures, a scourge in Kosovo, from taking hold.

Locals should be involved in decisionmaking as soon as possible. The presumption should always be to let locals assume responsibility, unless it becomes clear that they cannot or will not act with the requisite fairness and respect for human rights (e.g., local judiciary in Kosovo regarding ethnically related and other serious crimes). The UN should avoid acting like the "ugly imperialist" but also should not be reluctant to be assertive, even overriding local decisions. The odds of having to disagree with or veto local initiatives diminish the more carefully the UN has identified its local interlocutors or has allowed a broader swath of local society to choose intermediaries who represent a wide spectrum of society. Political correctness can boomerang.

Finally, the UN and other international actors should begin human rights education and promotion work right away. Here it is crucial to involve local partners in planning and setting priorities for reaching the local population. International actors should take a subordinate role, but this puts a premium on identifying and involving genuine local human rights experts.

* * *

José Ramos-Horta, the Nobel Prize–winning human rights activist and a leading voice of the East Timorese, was asked if all the violence and deaths that surrounded the August 31, 1999, referendum on independence "had been worth it." Ramos-Horta's answer was interesting. He said that if in five years there is tolerance for the minority Muslims and Protestants, if corruption is minimal, if there is an independent judiciary and a free press, and if the country will have eliminated malaria and tuberculosis, then all the death and destruction will have been worth it. Ramos-Horta added that after all the help, support, and solidarity shown by the international community toward the East Timorese, this community has earned the right to scrutinize and criticize the government if it failed to promote tolerance and respect for human rights.

While East Timor is different, a similar question must be asked of Kosovo. Also, we must ask whether UNMIK and NATO have effectively tackled Kosovo's underlying problems and, especially, have created conditions for tolerance across ethnic lines. The test for Kosovars, UNMIK, and NATO is not only "We must be better than the Milosevic regime was." That is too easy. Rather, in five years, if Kosovo does not have a free and responsible press, low corruption, an effective and rights-respecting police force, an independent judiciary, and, most important, a society that respects its minorities and embraces tolerance, then one would have to wonder whether the intervention and the follow-on work of UNMIK and NATO were worth it. And just as for East Timor, those running Kosovo— Kosovars, UNMIK, and NATO leaders—should welcome international scrutiny and, if warranted, criticism, because this right has been earned.

The record on both questions so far, as I have tried to describe, is mixed. The changes in Serbia with the removal of Milosevic, the triumph of Kostunica, and the strengthening of democracy give hope, just as the clear-cut victory of Rugova's party in Kosovo's elections underscore the basic decency, moderation, and desire for peace among the majority of Kosovo Albanians.

Hard-liners in both camps, however, have their own agendas. Former UCK and the UCPMB insurgents in southern Serbia illustrate the power of organized groups who do not hesitate to use violence. International criminal networks and trafficking in women thrive in Kosovo and threaten its security. Serb extremists in northern Kosovo still dream of reestablishing Serbian rule in a territory where Serbs are a tiny minority. And the conflict in Macedonia, initiated by the shadowy Albanian National Liberation Army, threatens to destabilize not only Macedonia but also Kosovo and Serbia proper. This army is an off-shoot of the UCK.[1]

Ramos-Horta's question will most likely be answered in the affirmative if young people like the ones in the Youth Group of Magura have their say. This group, in a small, run-down town in central Kosovo, refused to affiliate with the various Kosovo Albanian parties despite steady demands and pressure, insisting on being nonpolitical. The group keeps its focus on issues relevant to teenagers these days in Kosovo. They worry about drugs; more and more of their friends are experimenting and there is no formal program in the schools on the dangers of drug abuse. The same is true for alcohol and tobacco, and they have seen the ravages of both in their own families. HIV/AIDS is a growing problem in Kosovo, and the kids would like some useful education on this and other sexually transmitted diseases.

But most impressive of all, the youth of Magura are ready to start a serious dialogue on interethnic relations. They say it is stupid to like or dislike someone because of his or her ethnic background. They wonder whether Kosovo can possibly enter the twenty-first century as long as such medieval attitudes prevail. They want to meet with Serb, Bosniak, and Roma teenagers to discuss issues that interest all of them; they want to play soccer, listen to rock and "techno" music, and just hang out with all kinds of kids. When the day arrives that this dream comes true, then the intervention truly will have been worth it.

NOTE

1. Nick Wood, "Macedonian Troops Fight Albanian Rebels in Border Village," *Guardian Weekly,* March 1–7, 2001, p. 2.

Acronyms

AAK	Kosovo Alliance for the Future
ADJ	Administrative Department of Judicial Affairs (UNMIK)
CIVPOL	International Civilian Police (UN)
DPA	Department of Political Affairs (UN)
DPKO	Department of Peacekeeping Operations (UN)
EU	European Union
FRY	Federal Republic of Yugoslavia
FYROM	Former Yugoslav Republic of Macedonia
HRD	Human Rights Division (OSCE)
ICRC	International Committee of the Red Cross
ICTY	International Criminal Tribunal for the Former Yugoslavia
JAC/PJA	Joint Advisory Council on Provisional Judicial Appointments
KCS	Kosovo Correctional Service
KFOR	Kosovo Force (NATO)
KPS	Kosovo Police Service
KVM	Kosovo Verification Mission (OSCE)
LDK	Democratic League of Kosovo
LSMS	Legal Systems Monitoring Section (OSCE)
MNB	Multinational Brigade (NATO)
MUP	Yugoslav Ministry of Interior Police
NATO	North Atlantic Treaty Organization
NGO	nongovernmental organization
OHCHR	Office of the High Commissioner for Human Rights (UN)
OSCE	Organization for Security and Cooperation in Europe
PDK	Democratic Party of Kosovo
PU	UCK police
SRSG	special representative of the Secretary-General (UN)
TMK	Trupat Mbrojtese te Kosoves (Kosovo Protection Corps)
UCK	Ushtaria Climatare Kombetere (Kosovo Liberation Army)

UCPMB	Army for the Liberation of Presevo, Medvedja, and Bujanovac
UNHCHR	United Nations High Commissioner for Human Rights
UNHCR	United Nations High Commissioner for Refugees
UNICEF	United Nations Children's Fund
UNMIK	United Nations Interim Administration Mission in Kosovo
VJ	Vojska Jugoslavije (Yugoslav Armed Forces)
VRIC	Victim Recovery Identification Commission

Chronology of Key Events

1989
    March   Serbia revokes Kosovo's autonomous status.

1995
    November   Dayton Accords are signed ending the war in Bosnia.

1998
    March 3–5   First serious fighting takes place between Serbian forces and Kosovo Albanian insurgents; Jashari family is massacred by Serb forces in Drenica Valley.

    September 23   UN Security Council passes Resolution 1199 calling for the end of Serb forces attacks and the safe return of refugees.

    October 13   Milosevic agrees to the deployment of 2,000 unarmed observers from the OSCE in Kosovo (Kosovo Verification Mission, KVM).

    November 11   KVM begins operations.

1999
    January 15   Racak massacre occurs; Serb forces kill forty-five Albanians.

    February 6   Negotiations intended to end hostilities and determine the future status of Kosovo begin in Rambouillet, France.

    March 18   Talks collapse as Serbs refuse to sign final agreement.

    March 24   NATO bombing of Yugoslavia begins.

    May 7   NATO bombs Chinese Embassy in Belgrade.

    May 27   ICTY indicts Milosevic for war crimes in Kosovo.

1999

June 9	NATO and FRY sign Military-Technical Agreement; Serb forces agree to withdraw from Kosovo.
June 10	Bombing stops; Security Council passes Resolution 1244 creating UNMIK.
September 20	UCK formally disbands and is supposed to hand in weapons.
November 28	Albanian Flag Day is celebrated for the first time in ten years in Kosovo.
December 10–11	First International Human Rights Conference is held in Pristina.
December 15	SRSG announces Joint Administrative Structure for local governance.

2000

January	UCPMB, shadowy Albanian insurgent group, surfaces in Presevo Valley, Serbia proper.
January 21	TMK begins formal operations; leadership is sworn in.
February 4	Rocket attack is launched on a bus full of Serbs in a KFOR convoy; two Serbs are killed and many injured.
February 8	Eight Albanians are killed as violence flares in the divided city of Mitrovica.
June 2	Huge illegal weapons cache is discovered by KFOR 1 kilometer from TMK headquarters in Drenica Valley.
June 12	Date marks first anniversary of UNMIK.
September/October	Turmoil reigns in Serbia; elections yield Vojislav Kostunica as the new president; Slobodan Milosevic resigns.
October 28	Ibrahim Rugova's party wins convincingly in local elections in Kosovo.

2001

January 15	Hans Haekerrup becomes SRSG, replacing Bernard Kouchner.
February 16	Explosion destroys a bus full of Serbs in a KFOR convoy; eleven people are killed.
February/March	Insurgencies in Presevo Valley and Macedonia led by ethnic Albanians intensify.
March 12	Cease-fire is brokered by NATO between UCPMB and FRY forces.
March 14	FRY military return to buffer zone along Kosovo boundary between Macedonia and Serbia proper;

2001

	National Liberation Army in Macedonia continues fighting; hostilities spread to Tetovo area.
March 29	Fighting in Macedonia spills into Kosovo; three civilians are killed.
April 1	Milosevic is arrested in Belgrade.
April 25	Serb authorities release 143 Kosovo Albanians, who are originally from Djakovica, from detention in Serbia. They return home to a joyous welcome.
May 11	KFOR seizes a huge weapons cache in Kosovo destined for the ethnic Albanian rebels fighting in the Presevo Valley of southern Serbia.
May 14	UNMIK announces constitutional framework for self-rule and the date—November 17, 2001—for territory-wide elections.
May 22	UNMIK establishes new Pillar One responsible for police and the judiciary.
June 12	Thousands of Macedonian Albanians arrive in Kosovo, fleeing the fighting in Macedonia.
June 28	Serb authorities transfer Milosevic to the custody of the ICTY in The Hague.
July	Heavy fighting continues in Macedonia between the ethnic Albanian National Liberation Army (NLA) and Macedonian forces.
July 26	Four Kosovo Serb political parties agree to participate in November elections.
August 13	Cease-fire agreement is signed between Macedonian Albanian political leaders and the Macedonian government.
August 17	Advance team of NATO troops arrives in Macedonia to begin collecting weapons from the NLA as part of Operation Essential Harvest.

Selected Bibliography

Buckley, William J., ed. *Kosovo: Contending Voices on Balkan Interventions.* Grand Rapids, Mich.: Eerdmans Publishing, 2000.

Clark, Wesley G. *Waging Modern War.* New York: Public Affairs, 2001.

Daalder, Ivo, and Michael O'Hanlon. *Winning Ugly: NATO's War to Save Kosovo.* Washington, D.C.: Brookings Institution, 2000.

Doder, Dusko, and Louise Branson. *Milosevic: Portrait of a Tyrant.* New York: Free Press, 1999.

Glenny, Misha. *The Fall of Yugoslavia: The Third Balkan War,* 3d ed. New York: Penguin, 1996.

Human Rights Watch. *Kosovo: Rape as a Weapon of Ethnic Cleansing.* New York: Human Rights Watch, 2000.

Ignatieff, Michael. *Virtual War: Kosovo and Beyond.* New York: Henry Holt, 2000.

Judah, Tim. *Kosovo: War and Revenge.* New Haven: Yale University Press, 2000.

———. *The Serbs: History, Myth and the Destruction of Yugoslavia.* New Haven: Yale University Press, 1997.

Lawyers Committee for Human Rights. *A Fragile Peace: Laying the Foundations for Justice in Kosovo.* New York: Lawyers Committee for Human Rights, 1999.

Malcolm, Noel. *Kosovo: A Short History.* New York: New York University Press, 1999.

Mertus, Julie. *Kosovo: How Myths and Truths Started a War.* Berkeley: University of California Press, 1999.

Minear, Larry, Ted van Baarda, and Marc Sommers. *NATO and Humanitarian Action in the Kosovo Crisis.* Providence, R.I.: Thomas Watson Institute for International Studies, 2000.

Moore, Jonathan, ed. *Hard Choices: Moral Dilemmas in Humanitarian Intervention.* Lanham, Md.: Rowman and Littlefield Publishers, 1998.

Motes, Mary. *Kosovo/Kosova: Prelude to War, 1966–1999.* Homestead, Fla.: Redland Press, 1998.

OSCE. *Kosovo/Kosova: As Seen, As Told,* parts 1, 2. Warsaw: OSCE Office for Democratic Institutions and Human Rights, 1999.

Todorova, Maria. *Imagining the Balkans.* New York: Oxford University Press, 1997.

Vickers, Miranda. *Between Serb and Albanian: A History of Kosovo.* New York: Columbia University Press, 1998.

West, Rebecca. *Black Lamb and Grey Falcon: A Journey Through Yugoslavia.* New York: Penguin, 1994.

Woodward, Susan. *Balkan Tragedy: Chaos and Dissolution After the Cold War.* Washington, D.C.: Brookings Institution, 1995.

Index

About This Publication

Despite the deployment of NATO forces in Kosovo and the UN's direct involvement in governing the province, such terrors as murder, disappearances, bombings, and arson have become routine occurrences. William O'Neill analyzes the nature of the violence that continues to plague Kosovo's residents and assesses efforts to guarantee public security.

O'Neill considers how the particular evolution of the Kosovo Liberation Army has had enduring negative consequences for the rule of law, how weak UN and NATO policies have contributed to this trend, and how the situation might be reversed. The result is a unique window into a controversial peacekeeping mission, presented from a practitioner's point of view.

William G. O'Neill was senior adviser on human rights to the UN Interim Administration Mission in Kosovo (August 1999–February 2000). He has also served on human rights missions to Afghanistan, Bosnia-Herzegovina, Haiti, and Rwanda.

Other International Peace Academy Publications

Available from Lynne Rienner Publishers, 1800 30th Street, Boulder, Colorado 80301 (303-444-6684), www.rienner.com.

Rights and Reconciliation: UN Strategies in El Salvador, Ian Johnstone (1995)
Building Peace in Haiti, Chetan Kumar (1998)
Greed and Grievance: Economic Agendas in Civil War, edited by Mats Berdal and David M. Malone (2000)
The Sanctions Decade: Assessing UN Strategies in the 1990s, David Cortright and George A. Lopez (2000)
Peacebuilding as Politics: Cultivating Peace in Fragile Societies, edited by Elizabeth M. Cousens and Chetan Kumar (2001)
Sierra Leone: Diamonds and the Struggle for Democracy, John L. Hirsch (2001)
Toward Peace in Bosnia: Implementing the Dayton Accords, Elizabeth M. Cousens and Charles K. Cater (2001)
Civilians in War, edited by Simon Chesterman (2001)
Self-Determination in East Timor: The United Nations, the Ballot, and International Intervention, Ian Martin (2001)
Peacemaking in Rwanda: The Dynamics of Failure, Bruce D. Jones (2001)
From Reaction to Conflict Prevention: Opportunities for the UN System, edited by Fen Osler Hampson and David M. Malone (2002)
Building Peace in West Africa: Liberia, Sierra Leone, and Guinea-Bissau, Adekeye Adebajo (2002)

The International Peace Academy

The International Peace Academy (IPA) is an independent, nonpartisan, international institution devoted to the promotion of peaceful and multilateral approaches to the resolution of international as well as internal conflicts. IPA plays a facilitating role in efforts to settle conflicts, providing a middle ground where the options for settling particular conflicts are explored and promoted in an informal setting. Other activities of the organization include public forums; training seminars on conflict resolution and peacekeeping; and research and workshops on collective security, regional and internal conflicts, peacemaking, peacekeeping, and nonmilitary aspects of security.

In fulfilling its mission, IPA works closely with the United Nations, regional and other organizations, governments, and parties to conflicts. The work of IPA is further enhanced by its ability to draw on a worldwide network of eminent persons including government leaders, statesmen, business leaders, diplomats, military officers, and scholars. In the decade following the end of the Cold War, there has been a general awakening to the enormous potential of peaceful and multilateral approaches to resolving conflicts. This has given renewed impetus to the role of IPA.

IPA is governed by an international board of directors. Financial support for the work of the organization is provided primarily by philanthropic foundations, as well as individual donors.